The Magic of Bandelier

The Magic of

BANDELIER

David E. Stuart

Ancient City Press
Santa Fe, New Mexico

Cover design by Don Curry

Book design by Mary Powell

International Standard Book Number
Paperback 0-941270-56-4
Clothbound 0-941270-57-2
Library of Congress Catalogue Number
88-072050

Frontispiece: Bandelier National Monument: Frijoles Canyon looking upstream toward the Valle Caldera. Photo courtesy of the National Park Service, Bandelier National Monument, 1964.

Cover photograph: Aerial photograph of Tyonyi, in Frijoles Canyon, looking east. Photo courtesy of Baker Aero—Tom Baker, 1989.

For

Frederick A. Peterson
Field archeologist, friend, and author of Ancient Mexico

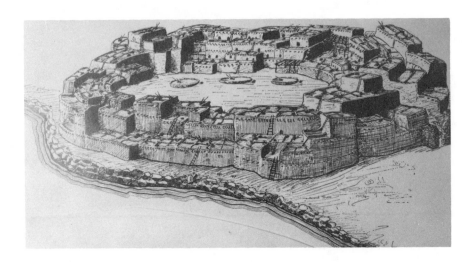

Artist's conception of Tyuonyi. This particular rendition makes the ruin look more massive than it probably was. Photo courtesy of the National Park Service, Bandelier National Monument.

Contents

Acknowledgments

I am grateful to Mary Powell and Marta Weigle of Ancient City Press for taking pains to produce a well-designed and edited volume and to Ms. Carla Warran at the University of New Mexico for typing from my difficult manuscript. We are grateful to Tom Baker for his stunning aerial photographs, and to Michael Marshall for the use of his own photographic "library" of ceramic artifacts. As most everyone who follows southwest archeology knows, Mike is not only a fine field archeologist, but an authority on regional pottery types—we use reproductions of his slides with great confidence that the reader will learn much from them. I also thank Rory P. Gauthier, archeologist at Bandelier National Monument, who first talked me into setting aside other book projects in order to write something special; then on his own time, he checked the manuscript for factual errors. Thanks also to the director and staff of Bandelier National Monument and especially to Ed Greene who suggested the most important guiding fact of all—that this book would usually be taken home by Monument visitors to be read at their leisure *after* visiting the Monument. Because of Ed's comment, I chose not to write a standard "guidebook" to sights, sounds, and trails, and indulged my considerable passion to guide visitors into a true understanding of just how Bandelier fits into a story six hundred human generations long.

Foreword

This "guidebook" is about the archeology of Bandelier National Monument. Bandelier has both a fascinating story to tell and a compelling sense of place which arises from that story. You will discover, however, that much of what archeologists know about Bandelier depends on events which happened to people centuries before and at substantial distances away from the modern monument. So learning about these, as you will in this book, is the only way to make good sense of the ruins found here.

There are other monuments, like Chaco Canyon, where the existing ruins are more awesome, and the ancient walls more elaborate. There are monuments, like the battlefield at Gettysburg, which are emotionally closer to many of us, pulling at our heartstrings and causing us to contemplate our very humanity. But Bandelier offers the visitor everything: intellectual stimulation, visual paradise, and a remarkably vibrant sense of peace. I am neither the first archeologist, nor the best to be enchanted with Frijoles Canyon. Yet I love it well enough to hope that this volume accurately captures its special essence. I always leave Bandelier feeling more peaceful than when I came. May you also.

David E. Stuart, January 1988
Albuquerque, New Mexico

PART I

THE MAGIC OF BANDELIER NATIONAL MONUMENT

Aerial photo of the Valle Caldera, showing most of the Valle Grande (foreground) and the East Fork of the Jemez River. Distant snow line is on the Sangre de Cristo Range across the Rio Grande Valley to the east and north. Photo courtesy of the National Park Service, Bandelier National Monument, 1964.

Frijoles Creek in winter. Tyuonyi is to the right, out of view. Photo courtesy of the National Park Service, Bandelier National Monument, 1978.

Introduction

The crowd gathers slowly. By twos and threes they file into the huge, darkened amphitheater at Juniper Campground. Here, a mile and one-third above sea level, the night sky is breathtaking. Brilliant stars and the Milky Way's swirling arc of cloudy light mingle with the recorded flute music, composed, perhaps, a thousand years ago.

This is Bandelier National Monument—fascinating by day, nightfall transforms it into an ancient and radiant natural theatre. The crowd is hushed. Some turn to watch flashlights twinkling along nearby paths as latecomers arrive from surrounding campgrounds. Kids snuggle under blankets, quietly awaiting the promised Friday night campfire lecture. British accents carry softly from the second row of wooden bleachers. To the right there is a friendly twang, typical of South Texas or Louisiana. Connecticut's clipped vowels are out there, too, but hidden in the dark. One kid in the front row, who wears his baseball cap sideways, gapes in awe as Sari Stein lights a bonfire at the amphitheater's edge, then comes to sit in the front row with her tape recorder. In the summer months she arranges speaker's programs for the Monument. Tonight, the topic is a regional favorite—"New Mexico's Archeological Heritage."

As the flute music stops, the rustic stone stage is lit and Rory Gauthier, a ranger at the Monument, steps up to introduce a local archeologist brought in to lecture. Rory first brings the hushed crowd back to earth with some anecdotes, welcomes them to the Monument, then gives them a brief background to the scheduled lecture. He neglects to mention that he has coauthored a substantial college text on Southwestern archeology, was born and raised in Los

Alamos, and knows more about the archeology of the surrounding area than all but four or five living scholars. Rory is modest.

Next comes the story of prehistoric Bandelier. The earliest villages in Bandelier National Monument were built by descendants of the Chaco-Anasazi whose basin-land towns were abandoned about eight hundred years ago. Drought brought these hardy Anasazi farmers into cool-forested highlands where rainfall is greater than in the lowlands and heavy winter snows feed crystal-clear streams in nearly every canyon. Bandelier's earliest pueblos, built in the late A.D. 1100s, were small, numerous and widely scattered. Times were hard, for cold nighttime temperatures prevented abundant harvests, and many villagers starved.

In the early thirteenth century, Bandelier's Indian people gathered into the first large cliff dwellings, abandoning the earlier outlying pueblos. Throughout these canyons, cliff dwellings faced south to catch the winter sun; their back rooms were often cut into the soft volcanic tuff of the mesas overlooking sparkling creeks. Above the Monument's headquarters, "cave rooms" line the main wall of Frijoles Canyon where the countless fist-sized socket holes were supports for roof beams, or vigas.

During the late A.D. 1200s a dependable water supply was of utmost importance to the Indians. Because Frijoles Creek ran year-round, this canyon was a perfect place for a village. The huge, circular structure of Tyuonyi (Chew-OHN-yee) grew until it was two or three stories tall and contained more than four hundreds rooms. Founded just before A.D. 1300, it prospered into the early 1500s, then was abandoned when Pueblo people concentrated their settlements along the Rio Grande Valley, a few miles to the east. Descendants of Tyuonyi, Keresan language speakers, still inhabit the Rio Grande Pueblos of Cochiti, Santo

4

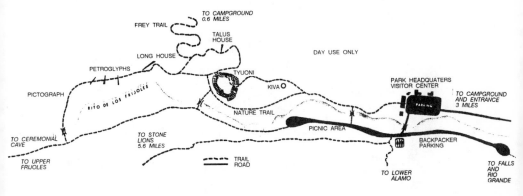

FRIJOLES CANYON

Domingo, and San Felipe.

As the lecture ends, a young woman asks what eventually became of those who inhabited the other ruined villages all around. The lecturer tells her that as many as half of Bandelier's ancient population died out during the two difficult centuries between A.D. 1100 and 1300. The story of New Mexico's heritage is one of pain and hardship, but also one of ingenuity, faith and hope—all keys to the triumph of Pueblo Indian survival.

After more questions and several favorite anecdotes, the crowd drifts away, flashlights twinkling. Later, a meteor shower explodes above the starlit north rim of Frijoles Canyon. Below, the night breeze wanders gently among great Ponderosas while Frijoles Creek rushes downhill to the Rio Grande. By dawn its passing waters will have given yet another day's precious life to someone's modern cornfields.

TRAIL MAP
BANDELIER
NATIONAL MONUMENT

0   1   2   3
SCALE IN MILES

SANTA FE NATIONAL FOREST

TO JEMEZ SPRINGS

N

S.R. 4

DEPARTMENT OF ENERGY

S.R. 501

LOS ALAMOS

S.R. 502

OTOWI

TO SANTA FE
S.R. 502

SANDIA

TSANKAWI

TSIREGE

WHITE ROCK

PONDEROSA
CAMPGROUND

FRIJOLES

UPPER
FRIJOLES
CROSSING

FRIJOLES CANYON

CREEK

S.R. 4

S.R. 4

JUNIPER
CAMPGROUND

TYUONYI

CEREMONIAL CAVE
LONG HOUSE

VISITOR CENTER

FRIJOLITO

TO S.R. 4

BOUNDARY PEAK

STONE LIONS

YAPASHI

RAINBOW
HOUSE

LOWER
FRIJOLES
CROSSING

RIO

GRANDE

ST. PETER'S DOME

DOME ROAD

BLAND CANYON ROAD

SAN MIGUEL

PAINTED CAVE

KIVA
HOUSE

COCHITI LAKE

○ MODERN CITIES
• RUINS
△ CAMPGROUNDS AND
   VISITOR'S FACILITIES
━━━ PAVED ROADS
━ ━ ━ UNPAVED ROADS
- - - TRAILS

MONUMENT IS SHADED AREA

The Special Character of Ancient Places

In the Southwest, there are a number of well-known monuments to prehistoric Indian society. Bandelier is a very special one, and, for travelers, a natural gateway to the rest:
Wupatki and Montezuma's Castle are a day's drive to the
west; two hundred miles to the north lies Mesa Verde; the
Gila Cliff Dwellings are three hundred miles to the south.
These monuments consist of ruined buildings, silent piles of
mud and stone. Each one is important for its own distinct
chapter in the story of Pre-Columbian society in America.
Each has a special personality, forged from its own lingering
sense of place and time in the flow of human events.

Wupatki, near Sunset Crater, Arizona, is compelling in
its desolation. Desert winds blow around impressive, well-
laid, well-preserved masonry walls. The adjacent slopes of
Sunset Crater are still and barren. Only the black sands and
fine pebbles shift ever so slightly in the ceaseless wind. It is
almost as if Wupatki were the prehistoric counterpart to
western ghost towns as portrayed in modern movies—the
wind, dust, bare walls, and empty buildings are haunted
only by the faint echoes of voices long gone. The whole
scene is desolate and forlorn.

Mesa Verde is different. It is both a natural and a cultural wonder. Verdant hills, snow-capped mountains, and
high, wooded mesas are a natural picture frame for the
almost perfect cliff ruins. Mughouse and Cliff Palace, like all
the major ruins at Mesa Verde, are neat, compact, logical,
and well-built. Set against soaring cliff faces, they are nearly
everyone's idea of the grandest villages in the prehistoric
Southwest. But those who built Mesa Verde have left too
many unanswerable questions: where and who are their

descendants; who were the builders; what languages did they speak; what names did they call themselves? Archeologists do not know for certain, so Mesa Verde, grand as it is and for all its magnificent cliff palaces, is really like a half-written chapter in an old history book. It is about yesterdays.

The Gila Cliff Dwellings are shady, quiet and enigmatic. In A.D. 1200 this was the only "cliff palace" in southern New Mexico. Some Anasazi from west-central New Mexico moved south after the Chaco decline and took up a precarious existence, surrounded by remnants of Mogollon society. They abandoned the cliff dwelling in the late A.D. 1200s. No one knows where they went, or why they came so far south in the first place. This place is a puzzle.

Then there is Chaco Canyon National Historical Park. At Chaco the timeless desert-blue sky hangs above rock and sage, stunted juniper, red-brown earth and red-brown buildings. Best known is Pueblo Bonito with its 332 ground-floor rooms, circular kivas, and banded masonry walls still partially standing. Row upon row of sandstone slabs were laboriously hand chinked with millions of small stone chips. The meticulous beauty of its masonry is unequalled anywhere north of Mexico.

Chaco Canyon's persona is awesome, radiating a sense of power. In its heyday, the inhabitants of Pueblo Bonito surely believed fervently in its potency. Even the great broken crag of Threatening Rock, braced up in prehistoric times, did not dare to fall and crush the rear of Pueblo Bonito until the afternoon of January 21, 1941—eight hundred years after its abandonment. This one village symbolizes ancient North America's greatest political and economic power. Pueblo Indian peoples alive today all claim to be descended from those who built Pueblo Bonito.

Chaco Canyon creates strong emotions in the traveler,

Cliff Palace at Mesa Verde, Colorado. Photo by Jesse L. Nusbaum, 1907. Courtesy of Museum of New Mexico, negative number 60649.

but one is never more than a visitor. For outsiders there is no sense of belonging. Pueblo Bonito and Chaco Canyon belong—have always belonged—to the souls of those who built it and lived in it. The raw power of Chaco Canyon is seductive to a modern society obsessed with power, but it does not share its power with visitors of any kind.

Bandelier National Monument is quite different from these other Southwest ruins. Perhaps it is simply the crystalline air, 7000 feet above sea level. Perhaps the remarkable views across the mesas, or the homeyness of Juniper Campground, or the solitude of the trail to the Stone Lions make Bandelier friendlier and more peaceful. Perhaps the special emotional appeal comes from the story of Bandelier—the saga of the people here yesterday, today, and tomorrow.

The bottom of Frijoles Canyon behind the Visitor Center's gallery is remarkably restful. There the traveler enters a magical world where great tuff cliffs, shadow-framed cave rooms and immense rock promontories all jut up toward the heavens. Even the sky on the Pajarito Plateau seems a purer shade of turquoise than at any other place on earth.

The seasons are also special at Bandelier. Each night in late summer a chill breeze rises gently up the canyon, smelling of autumn even before it arrives. In winter, at Painted Cave, the midday sun heats ancient rock with the delicate warmth of a coming spring. On a bright springtime morning atop the higher mesas, warmed air, rising from black basalt cliffs near the Rio Grande, creates a gentle breeze over the lip of the mesas. These breezes carry the sharp scent of pine needles in anticipation of summer. It is a subtle place, alive with changing shadows, unexpected colors, and its own private seasons. Sunlight yesterday, rain today, snow tomorrow.

From behind the Visitor's Center, facing west, the view

is up the canyon towards the ruins of Tyuonyi. The oldest ruins lie even further up-canyon—the Bandelier of yesterdays. The Depression Era Visitors Center is full of life and color. Its shaded courtyards and verandas accommodate crowds of visitors year-round. It is the Bandelier of today. As one travels down Frijoles Canyon, each ruin is newer than the last until one arrives in the contemporary Rio Grande Indian Pueblos. Their unborn generations will continue to venerate the ancient shrines above Frijoles Canyon—this is the Bandelier of tomorrow.

The Monument's name is a special story, too. A little over a century ago, Adolph Bandelier, accompanied by his Cochiti Indian guides, came over a rugged, long-abandoned trail, to look down into Frijoles Canyon. It was October of 1880 and he was no longer young—like Frijoles Canyon, Bandelier had already experienced his yesterdays. Born in Switzerland in the summer of 1840, he came to the United States as a boy. Later, his family settled near St. Louis. Adolph spent his early adulthood miscast, bored and unfulfilled, working in his father's banking business.

When he first came to Frijoles Canyon at the age of forty, Bandelier had left behind the security of a family business and a conventional way of life. These days a psychologist would probably diagnose this behavior as a "mid-life crisis." Whatever his motives, it is singularly fortunate that a true romantic stepped to the rim of the canyon on that October day and looked down on the ruins now called Tyuonyi. In that instant, Bandelier the anthropologist was captivated by the area's special magic.

Adolph Bandelier did much for anthropology, not as an original researcher, but as a meticulous observer who brought both true passion and perceptive vision to this work. The rest of his life was primarily spent studying prehistoric societies, always with a spirit of romance. The twelve years he actually spent in the Southwest, though interrupted by his travels to Europe and Mexico, were from 1880 to 1892. That is a singular, if not stunning, coincidence for it was precisely two hundred years before that the great Pueblo Revolt of 1680-1692 had driven every Spaniard from the Rio Grande south into what is now Old Mexico. During those twelve years, New Mexico's Pueblo Indian peoples tried one last time to reestablish the "old ways" that had existed before Spanish colonization in 1598. Two centuries later, Bandelier came as if on a schedule designed to commemorate the Pueblo society he was destined to immortalize.

Most modern-day anthropologists would not approve of Bandelier's research methods. In the late nineteenth century, the field of archeology was still in its infancy. The techniques of excavation were just becoming organized and systematic, as were the identification and classification of differing pottery styles. However, most of these developments were taking place in Europe and the Middle East at famous sites like Troy, Ur of the Chaldees, and the Great Pyramids in Egypt. Obviously, Bandelier would not have been on the forefront of technique in scientific methodology. Instead Bandelier's unique contribution to the Monument that bears his name was fascination, a fascination for Indian society that was nearly obsessive. His intense inquisitiveness, coupled with a prodigious ability to read, assimilate information, and fastidiously record all that he heard and saw, gave us his spectacular *Journals*. These volumes, carefully edited and annotated in modern times, are still a valuable reference for Pueblo Indian society and the many ancient ruins Bandelier visited a century ago.

Adolph Bandelier left us more than his scholarly journals. In 1890 he needed money, so he wrote a novel portraying life in Frijoles Canyon as he reconstructed it from his studies. His book, *The Delight Makers*, not quite fact and not quite fiction, may well be one of the first written in the increasingly popular "modern" style now called "faction." *The Delight Makers* was both a commercial and a literary success. It is still available new, in almost any bookstore specializing in the southwest. Precious few books remain in print a century, so it has become a true classic. The very title, *The Delight Makers*, captures the special character of Bandelier National Monument. Adolph Bandelier understood, a century ago, that Frijoles Canyon and the Pajarito Plateau are not like the Chaco country. Chaco Canyon is a restless sky, a whirlwind of dust, a place not at peace with itself, even after eight centuries without inhabitants. In contrast, Frijoles Canyon is full of quiet sunlight, curious animals, little birds and peaceful innocence. It is a place where "delight makers" truly could have once walked the earth.

Adolph Bandelier's later years were caught up in the unusual sense of flowing time that is often experienced in Frijoles Canyon. He left his family and business in Illinois, to explore and discover all that he could of prehistoric life in the Southwest. During his years in New Mexico, Bandelier seemed to experience a heightening of all his senses. He saw, smelled, tasted, touched, heard, and dreamed with unusual clarity, recording most of it for posterity. Then, as now, New Mexico was a remarkable place, full of sights, sounds, and people quite exotic to a Midwesterner.

Bandelier died in comparative poverty while in Seville, Spain, just as World War I began in 1914. He was doing research in the magnificent Archives of the Indies, his dream of many years. Nearly three-quarters of a century after his death his ashes were finally scattered over the Monument which carries his name.

Visitors to Bandelier National Monument have a very special opportunity to understand, appreciate, and respect the human saga that took place there. They are free to smell, to look, to listen, and to savor all the delights that the monument holds. For the archeologist, these delights come primarily from rediscovering the past. For the visitor, the sheer beauty and the sense of peace are long remembered.

But Bandelier Monument was not created just because of its natural beauty and its unusual flow of seasons. It was created to celebrate, protect, and preserve the cultural treasures of the people who once lived in it—people whose descendants still live nearby in New Mexico. Unlike Wupatki, unlike Mesa Verde, unlike Chaco Canyon, unlike Gila Cliff Dwellings and most of the rest, Bandelier is not a dusty page already closed on the past. It is a window where one can look back into yesterday or enjoy today or dream about a thousand summers from now. Even archeologists, like Monument visitors, are struck by this sensation of past and future: from Tyuonyi's circular ruins they also look to the high, western mesas with even older ruins, many of them uncharted; to the east, they look down the canyon, where there are newer ruins along the Rio Grande, and beyond to the modern-day Pueblos.

As this volume is being written, a new and exciting chapter in the archeology of Bandelier National Monument is beginning. For the first time, government archeologists are attempting to survey major portions of the Monument on foot in order to locate and record all the different kinds of archeological remains—large and small. The Monument is just over fifty square miles in area. Modern computations of the number of archeological sites per square mile (each 640 acres) indicate that the minimum number of ruins in the Monument is well over a thousand. Just two years ago, the estimate was only half that number, but about eight hundred are known today. As many as 3000 archeological sites eventually could be found in the Monument, spanning all time periods from 10,000 B.C. to A.D. 1600.

A number of archeologists currently believe that most of the ruins yet to be found will belong to essentially the same time period as Tyuonyi and Rainbow House Ruin, a half mile down the canyon from the Visitor's Center on the north bank of Frijoles Creek. This author takes the view that, over the years, there are going to be some tantalizing discoveries from many time periods. This likelihood is based on recent evidence from archeological research projects in adjacent areas that are just like Monument lands in terms of topography and geography.

The Pajarito Plateau actually covers more than 300 square miles. It is bisected, east-to-west, by a whole series of deep canyons with high mesas between. On nearly every mesa there are ancient ruins; and in each canyon there are even more ruins. So, Bandelier Monument is, in fact, a largely unexplored archeological preserve, one-sixth of the Pajarito, which lies in the midst of proven archeological resources.

The ancient peoples of the Pajarito came and went for thousands of years, and their discarded artifacts—pottery, bits of stone, occasionally an arrowhead—can be found virtually anywhere in the Monument. Examples of these can be seen in the displays at the Visitor's Center. It is against the law to move or take artifacts, and worse, it destroys the past. Some archeological sites will be marked only by a dozen pottery fragments each the size of a thumbnail. Removing any of them can forever destroy the ability of a field archeologist to assign an accurate date to that site.

Modern archeologists seldom carry away artifacts, either. They regularly determine the general age of a ruin by looking at only a dozen or two dozen fragments of pottery. They will mark a fragment, pick it up, look at it under a hand lens, record the characteristics on long, complex "field forms," then put it back on its original site, unless they are taking a formal "type" collection for later analytical purposes.

The loss of just a few shards, sometimes even one, on a site can strip away all the artifacts that can be assigned a relatively well-defined age. Stone tools are even harder to date, since a particular type often lasted hundreds, even thousands, of years. Without pottery, there is often nothing for an archeologist to see, save a low mound. At other sites, particularly ancient pithouses, there are no rough block walls at all; only the faintest depression in the soil and a half-dozen fragments of dirty, gray pottery mark the site. Often, without the pottery clues, the pithouse sites, filled in by centuries of erosion, are too subtle for even the sharpest-eyed archeologist to notice.

The potential for discovery in Bandelier is remarkable and exciting. Many scholars doubt that, even a century from now, the final story on the archeology of Bandelier will have been written. Some archeologists maintain that there are no Archaic Period sites, those dating from roughly 5000 B.C. to A.D. 300 or 400, in the Monument. Others think there are, since they have been excavated in the lower elevations, now under Cochiti Reservoir. Some scholars say there were no very early pithouse dwellers in the Monument—during the period between A.D. 400 and A.D. 800 or 900. But, elsewhere in the Southwest, ancient people had already settled into modest pithouse villages in cool ponderosa country quite similar to Bandelier's.

In the Jemez high country, within twenty miles of Bandelier, where thickets of oak form along the creeks or on protective ridges, there are many small, one-hand grinding stones, which were once used to mash acorns. These are often found littering the landscape near dense stands of Gambels oak, so some should turn up in the monument itself. These smooth brown stream cobbles, shaped like a large aspirin, could be the clue needed to fill in a sketchy chapter in Bandelier's long saga.

Whether one visits Bandelier Monument to discover—to look into the past—or merely to seek peace, it is a place of timeless beauty all around. Its high mesas look east toward the Sangre de Cristo Mountains. Below them lies Santa Fe and yet another chapter in New Mexico's long history. From Bandelier's unique vistas one can look to the past, down to today's busy world or imagine yet another six hundred generations of life to come. That is the special magic of Bandelier.

PART II

ARCHEOLOGY:
THE CHAPTERS OF A HUMAN SAGA

Cave Kiva. Photo courtesy of the National Park Service, Bandelier
National Monument.

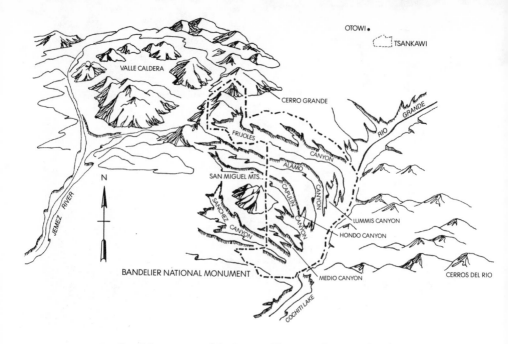

Profile of the canyons of the Pajarito Plateau as shown in the photograph on facing page. Drawing courtesy of Bandelier National Monument, National Park Service.

Bandelier National Monument tilts eastward toward the rising sun. Its fifty-square miles of rugged canyon and mesa lands sweep upward from the mile-high Rio Grande on the east to the summit of Cerro Grande (10,190 feet) on the north.

Natural historians think of Bandelier as a particular site on the east face of the Jemez Mountains atop a sloping bench known as the Pajarito (little bird) Plateau. Much of this rocky shelf was formed by the deep layers of volcanic tuff, or hardened ash, which exploded from the Jemez volcano (now a volcanic cone, or *Caldera*) more than a million years ago.

Archeologists, on the other hand, think of Bandelier National Monument as a concentrated island of archeological treasures in the vast landscape of the Great Southwest

20

Aerial view of the Pajarito Plateau with the Rio Grande in the fore-ground. Photo courtesy of Baker Aero—Tom Baker, 1989.

where more than 100,000 sites are known. It was established in 1916 primarily to celebrate and promote Tyuonyi, the spectacular circular ruins in Frijoles Canyon. Most of the nearby "cliff houses" were built sometime between the early 1200s and 1400s A.D., so older guidebooks often give the impression that Bandelier only figures into several centuries of prehistoric southwestern life. But artifacts found on the Monument include those from every major cultural horizon in New Mexico: Paleo-Indian (about 9,500 B.C. to 5,500 B.C.); the Archaic (about 5,000 B.C. to the birth of Christ); the Basketmaker (about A.D. 300 to about 800); and Pueblo (about A.D. 800 to 1600). True, the Monument's heyday was between A.D. 1150 and 1350, but the human saga first unfolds there nearly six hundred human generations ago.

Classic Hunter - Gatherer Society
The Paleo-Indian Period

Ancestors of Bandelier's first toolmakers almost certainly came to the Americas from northern Asia across a narrow corridor of dry land between Siberia and Alaska. During the last great ice age (the Pleistocene), when huge amounts of sea water were frozen into glacial ice packs, sea levels dropped. Most scholars currently believe America was first populated between fifteen and forty thousand years ago by small, successive migrations of nomadic hunters following animal herds. These long-vanished peoples left only poorly-dated traces of their campsites on this continent, but we know that they already possessed fire and made a variety of stone tools before reaching Alaska. Their descendants soon developed finely-flaked, fluted lance heads of remarkable quality. Since archeologists know nothing of their language, their names for themselves, or other details of daily life, they are collectively called "Paleo-Indians" (Old Indians) wherever their stone tools are found. `

No one knows precisely when they first came to the Southwest, but the earliest campsites to be well-dated appear between 9,000 and 10,000 B.C. By 9,500 B.C., the first documented groups of these hunters were living in present-day New Mexico. Their camps, known as "Clovis" sites, are named for their distinctive fluted stone lance heads, first found near Clovis, New Mexico, 250 miles east-southeast of the Pajarito Plateau.

Clovis lance heads, nine to ten thousand years old, have been found in Bandelier Monument. Several of these were made of Pedernal chert, a type of stone obtained nearby; others are of cherts from the high plains of Texas. Just how many Clovis tool makers lived in or around the

Monument is unclear since archeologists have paid little attention to these finds. Archeologists are convinced that most Clovis hunters were plains dwellers. Many larger Clovis sites are found on the rolling plains of New Mexico to the east of the monument.

As the last ice age was slipping away 10,000 years ago, summers were 11° cooler, on average, than nowadays. Tall stands of Ponderosa grew 500-to 1000-feet lower than where they are found today, so Frijoles Canyon would have been far more densely wooded. Summers were particularly cool and wet and the seasons were not so well-defined. Long-extinct megafauna (giant animals) still roamed New Mexico: mastodons, dire wolves, giant ground-sloths and camels all co-existed with these early nomads. Probably there were very few people at any one time in the lowlands below Bandelier; life was an endless trek from campsite to campsite as small family bands followed game, gathering favorite berries along the way. Still, Clovis craftsmen made their beautiful tools, exercising particularly remarkable control over the thickness and width of the lance head base. This was important in hafting them securely to socketed wood or bone fore-shafts.

Clovis hunters were also quite choosy about the stone from which their lance heads were made. Favored stone quarries have been identified at several places in Texas and at Sapello, near Las Vegas, New Mexico. Lance heads from these sources are often found hundreds of miles from the quarries; local stone was used only when stone from favorite sources was unavailable. Since lance heads of both local and imported stone have been found in Bandelier, either permanent local populations of Clovis hunters frequented the area or eastern plainsmen stayed long on high-country hunts, exhausting their supplies of the treasured eastern stone. Either way, the use of local stone indicates Bandelier

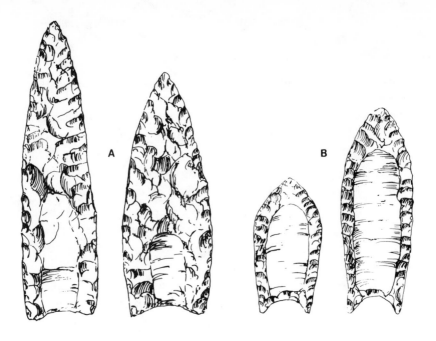

A   B

was an important hunting ground.

Later Paleo-Indian lance heads have also been found, among them Folsom (7,000 to 8,000 B.C.) and Scottsbluff (about 6,500 B.C.). Folsom lance heads were also fluted, but of even finer workmanship than the earlier Clovis ones, while the later Scottsbluff were carefully-flaked long blades and had no flute. Buffalo was the favored large game for both Folsom and Scottsbluff hunters. By later Paleo-Indian times, the climate had changed to more moderate conditions and the giant Ice Age mammals had vanished. By then the tall ponderosa grew only on the high mesas, while pinon and juniper were found on lower ones just as they are today.

Most sites of these early periods are found in New Mexico's open grasslands which are lower in elevation than Bandelier Monument. There bison lived in huge, migratory herds. In some seasons, or in poor years, there might have been no bison at all in the lowlands east of the Pajarito. In those times, upland species such as deer, elk, and bighorn

c

Prehistoric points: a. Clovis, b. Folsom, c. Scotts-bluff. Clovis Points, named after finds near Clovis, N.M., are the earliest well-dated tools in North America—about 10,000 B.C. These distinctive, bayonet-grooved Folsom lanceheads date to about 9,000 B.C. and were the first prehistoric tools found imbedded in the bones of extinct bison—conclusive proof that humans had inhabited New Mexico long before the Christian Era. The long, elegantly flaked "Scotts-bluff" knives and Eden lanceheads were remarkably efficient tools used in the "Cody" Period of the great buffalo hunts about 5,500 B.C. From *Prehistory of the Southwest* by Linda Cordell 1984, courtesy of Academic Press Inc.

sheep would have been the important sources of meat, hides, and bone. Then as now, the deep canyons in Bandelier Monument—Frijoles, Alamo and Capulin—would have provided game, fine campsites, and water.

Only isolated lance heads of the Paleo-Indian era have been found, which is not surprising, for these ancient people required vast territory for foraging. But some archeologists believe that true campsites will eventually be found near the Rio Grande in one of Bandelier's many canyons. The habits of later Apache bands is suggestive. Among these nineteenth century hunters it was common to gather for buffalo hunts in late spring or mid-fall. After a successful hunt, the large parties scattered and small family groups sought sheltered canyons to prepare winter camps. The Monument area itself offers such campsites but would not have supported more than three or four Paleo-Indian families at any one time.

Lavish Use of Landscapes
The Archaic Period

The era of Paleo-Indian hunters ended when climate again changed dramatically. It became hotter and drier, a period climatologists call the Altithermal (roughly 5,000 B.C. to 3,000 B.C.). Bison evolved into successively smaller subspecies as the Southwest became more arid. Then local bison became scarce or may have disappeared altogether as remnant herds sought refuge to the north in present-day Colorado, Wyoming, and the Dakotas.

By roughly 5,500 to 5,000 B.C. a wide region around Bandelier may have supported no humans at all. Several archeologists are convinced that the harsh, dry altithermal caused such a situation. Other scholars maintain that remnant populations hung on and were eventually augmented by migrations of neighboring Indian peoples into New Mexico. Whatever the case, a new style of living grew up in New Mexico beginning around 4,800 B.C. Characterized by far more intensive use of wild vegetal resources and by much less wandering, this is simply called the Archaic (Ancient) Period.

Until 1931, there was no conclusive proof of the earlier Paleo-Indian peoples, so the first anthropologists who worked at Bandelier, including Adolph Bandelier himself, believed that no humans had lived in the Americas much before the Christian Era. Even then the Archaic Period attracted little interest; investigations focused on the several centuries when cave rooms, cliff houses, and the well-known villages in Frijoles Canyon were inhabited. This emphasis has not changed in the intervening century.

Lance heads, dart points and knives (often mistaken for arrowheads) of the various Archaic periods are found in the

Jay point, length, 7.3 cm. (Illustrated by Charles M. Carrillo.) Jay points are typical of the early Archaic Period about 4,000 B.C. They are frequently found in and around Bandelier and are often fashioned of fine-grained black basalt quarried from the black, rocky mesas near the Rio Grande.

Monument. These include early types known as Jay and Bajada (5,000 -3,000 B.C.), and more numerous late Archaic tools (2,000 B.C. -A.D. 300). As with Paleo-Indian finds, these clues on the Pajarito Plateau have not been systematically pursued, but modern research into Archaic Period technology and economy has begun both to the west and the east of the Monument.

Looking south, down Alamo Canyon to White Rock Canyon and Cochiti Reservoir, it is possible to see La Bajada Mesa. During the Archaic Period, the Bajada Point, a stemmed lance head dating to about 3,000 B.C., was commonly made in the area. Most Bajada points were flaked from the black fine-grained to glassy basalt which forms the lower mesas that jut up from the Rio Grande. These mesas were laid down in a massive volcanic eruption earlier than the one which formed the higher, soft tuff mesas like those found on either side of Frijoles Canyon.

La Bajada Mesa and areas now submerged under Cochiti Reservoir supported increasing populations of Archaic peoples over the course of several thousand years.

Aerial photo of Alamo Canyon on the Pajarito Plateau. The entire Bandelier area is cross-cut by similar, deep canyons. Note the dramatic changes in vegetation and the relative "isolation" of the canyon floor. Photo courtesy of Baker Aero Works—Tom Baker, 1989.

The majority of identified sites are dated between 2,000 B.C. and A.D. 300. However, thirty miles to the west along the Rio Puerco, archeologist Cynthia Irwin-Williams identified *in situ* (in place) development of Archaic cultures beginning about 5,000 B.C. and continuing, unbroken, until just after the birth of Christ. The Rio Puerco cannot be seen from Bandelier because the rugged Jemez and Nacimiento Mountains cut off the view, but Bandelier was, and is, like a high, wooded promontory.

The Monument area was undoubtedly used throughout the Archaic Period, especially the lower elevations at the margin of present-day Cochiti Reservoir. Black, banded obsidian (volcanic glass) from the Polvadera Quarry and speckled varieties from Obsidian Ridge were used for three thousand years or more to fashion many of the lance heads,

1 through 7 are hammerstones unique to the Pajarito. 8 through 10 are one handed manos typical of the middle and late archaic and found in Bandelier area. Photo courtesy of Los Alamos National Laboratory.

knives and scrapers found locally. Jemez Mountain obsidian was employed with increasing frequency throughout the period. By the early Christian era, tools of Jemez obsidian were being used over thousands of square miles in north-central New Mexico.

As in Paleo-Indian times, the Monument's wooded mesas and sheltered canyons would have been important hunting territory for neighboring peoples. But Archaic people were, above all, plant collectors. Pinon nuts and Gambel's oak acorns would have been important sources of storable high-protein food to augment game taken in the harsh winters of northern New Mexico. West of the Monument, just across the Jemez, a recent archeological survey has discovered areas where Archaic people harvested acorns, then ground them into a protein-rich meal. They

Obsidian was mined along similar hills in the Valle Caldera over-looking a portion of the Valle Grande. Photo courtesy of the National Park Service, Bandelier National Monument, 1964.

left hundreds of their pill-shaped grinding stones, called one-handed manos, behind. Where these are found, there are also bedrock mortars— natural boulders pock-marked with distinctly unnatural circular depressions. These basin metates were created by the twisting, grinding motions of the Indian women, laboriously working their one-handed manos—the first effective "food-processor"! A concerted effort to find similar sites in the Monument itself has not been undertaken; it is likely that several grinding sites will eventually be found near some of the Monument's dense stands of oak and pinon.

By the end of Archaic times, in the early Christian era, local populations began to group themselves into small, scattered semi-permanent settlements. None of these settlements have been found on Monument lands, but wide, corner-notched lance heads of this period, called Basketmaker II points and shaped like the ace-of-spades, have been discovered here. Archeologists do agree that the areas to the south (near modern-day Jemez Pueblo), the west (the Rio Puerco Valley), and the east (Rio Grande Valley) all supported modest populations of part-time horticulturalists between 500 B.C. and A.D. 200-300. In the lowlands surrounding Bandelier, shallow (up to three feet deep) dugout pithouses and food storage cists were built even before fired pottery was manufactured. These early storage cists are simple, circular pits, often two-to-three feet across and lined with rough sandstone slabs.

Few people realize that early "farmers" in New Mexico continued to depend heavily on hunting and foraging some food supplies for more than a thousand years after corn was introduced from Mexico. The introduction of cultigens (corn, beans, and squash) didn't radically alter Archaic lifestyles for many generations. This first corn, called *chapalote*, was a very small-cobbed popcorn; crop yields were quite modest. Later, near the very end of the pre-pottery periods (about 300 B.C.), a larger cobbed corn with eight rows of kernels (*maiz de ocho*) was introduced into New Mexico, probably from northwest Mexico. This corn produced larger yields, and small garden plots of it became increasingly important during the early Christian era.

Many archeologists doubt that much more evidence of Archaic peoples will ever be found in Bandelier National Monument. Perhaps it was used only as a hunting territory and as a source of prized obsidian until long after nearby parts of New Mexico had been settled with the first tiny villages. Other scholars think many more discoveries will be made here, just as they have been in other areas of high-

Basket Maker II basket. A typical artifact before pottery was made in
Northern New Mexico, before A.D. 300. Blair Clark, photographer.
Courtesy of Utah collection in the Museum of New Mexico, catalog
number 43937/11, 1989.

canyon land throughout northern New Mexico. Prior to
1980, little systematic archeological investigation had even
been attempted above 6500 feet elevation. It was generally
believed that Paleo-Indian and Archaic peoples seldom ven-
tured into the higher woodlands. But, during the late 1970s
and early 1980s, a team of archeologists working for the
Bureau of Indian Affairs on potential timber-sale lands
found artifacts and small campsites of the pre-Christian era
in virtually *every* mountainous, timbered region where they
systematically hunted for traces of these early foragers.

Exploring Village Life
The Basketmaker Period

This period is known by several names because archeologists have identified several sub-periods as it has been studied. The name "Basketmaker" was first used by Richard Wetherill, the famous nineteenth-century rancher and explorer of Mesa Verde and Chaco Canyon, to describe the people and culture he found in Grand Gulch, Utah. There, early Indians made spectacular baskets and woven goods of all kinds. They were quite sophisticated weavers but did not yet manufacture pottery. They were also farmers, judging from corn cobs they had stored under dry rock overhangs.

In Bandelier Monument itself there is not much evidence of Basketmaker weaving or of the early pithouses they created, but stone tools have been recovered. Modest Basketmaker farmsteads of up to three pithouses have been excavated in adjacent lowlands along the Rio Grande, the Rio Puerco, and Jemez Creek.

Ojala Cave in Bandelier, near the margins of Cochiti Reservoir, was excavated a few years ago. Although no pithouses were found, there is evidence that this rock overhang was inhabited sporadically during a 2,500 year span from Archaic to Basketmaker times. A wide variety of stone tools and ancient seeds of numerous local plants eaten during prehistoric times have been recovered. Surprisingly sophisticated knowledge of seasonally available plants and animals is indicated by this find. It tells us, again, that wild food harvests continued to be important, even after corn was introduced.

The important story of the Basketmaker Period is that the pace of development was quite different from one region to another. The Bandelier area seems to have been tranquil at a time when powerful demographic forces brought radical change in village size, architecture and regional economics to the west and south. Unique regional cultures were developing in the Southwest; in a wide area around the Gila Cliff Dwellings National Monument Mogollon culture sprang up. The Mogollon made brown cooking pots instead of gray, indicating a fundamentally different ceramic technology. Their kivas were square, unlike the round ones of the Anasazi in northern New Mexico, and their social practices are believed to have differed substantially. The basin-lands surrounding Chaco Canyon were the location of classic Basketmaker villages, which, in turn, gave rise to Anasazi society.

Anasazi is a Navajo name given later to the vanished inhabitants of many ruins in the Chaco heartland. Most books translate it as "ancient ones," but a more accurate rendition would be "ancestors of the enemy," a reference to the often hostile relationship between Navajos and Pueblo peoples in early historic times. (In the Southwest, the "historic" period begins in 1540 with the written accounts of Coronado's expedition through Arizona and New Mexico.)

The saga of Bandelier is the story of the eastern Anasazi, farmers and settled villagers of the Four Corners region and northwestern New Mexico. Eastern Anasazi created the structures which are now ruins in Canyon De Chelly National Monument, Chaco Canyon National Historical Park, Aztec Ruins National Monument, El Morro National Monument, Bandelier National Monument, and Pecos National Monument. Each of these contributes a unique part to the archeological jigsaw puzzle which is reconstructing a picture of Anasazi development.

Anasazi culture began to develop in earnest about A.D. 400. The crude, scattered pithouses of the prepottery Basketmaker II period were replaced by larger, deeper, circu-

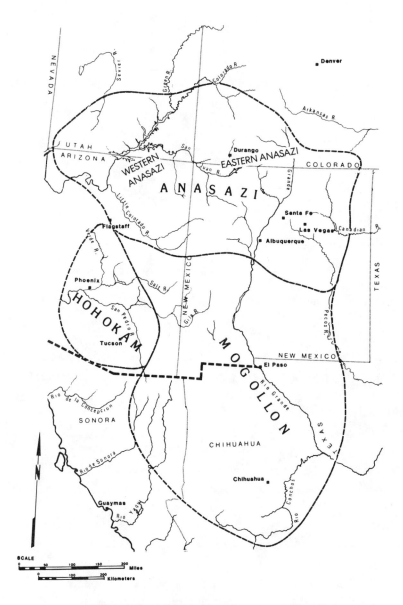

Map of Anasazi, Hohokam and Mogollon regions, From *Prehistory of the Southwest* by Linda Cordell 1984, Courtesy of Academic Press Inc.

White House Ruins at Canyon de Chelly. Photo by Ben Wittick.
Courtesy of the School of American Research Collections in the
Museum of New Mexico, negative number 15510.

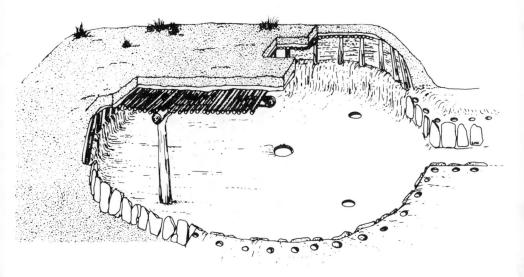

Artist's conception of a reconstructed pithouse. From *Prehistory of the
Southwest* by Linda Cordell 1984. Courtesy of Academic Press Inc.

lar pithouses with built-in firepits, rampway entrances
(usually facing east to catch the morning sun), large storage
bins, and subfloor cists. Pithouses were an extremely practical form of architecture. The earth was loosened with fire-
hardened digging sticks and crude stone hoes, then excavated with trough-shaped, rectangular cottonwood scoops.
The domed roofs were first timbered, then "shingled" with
saplings and boughs, and finally covered with the excavated
soil. Warm in winter and cool in summer, pithouses were as
efficient as any modern earth-bermed dwelling.

The first sizeable clusters of these pithouse farmsteads
were established primarily in well-watered areas near the
uplands and mountains surrounding the San Juan Basin
(present-day Four Corners area). Soon after, similar settlements were founded throughout the central basin in scattered areas of good soil with nearby seasonal streams or

Lino Gray Pot. An undecorated utility ware typical of early Basket-maker III (A.D. 400-700) in northern New Mexico. Photo courtesy of Mike Marshall, Maxwell Museum Collections.

springs. More modest versions of the San Juan Basin settlements ringed the Pajarito Plateau in adjacent lowlands.

The earliest pottery made in northern New Mexico was a plain, undecorated ware called Lino Gray. It is usually found mixed in with some of the brown clay cooking pots typical of southern New Mexico's Mogollon people. Archeologists have never agreed as to why these two fundamentally different pottery types are found together during this early period. To date neither of these ceramic styles has been found in the Monument. Apparently Bandelier's early inhabitants did not participate in the experimentation which led to the first settled agricultural villages to the south and west.

It was the western half of the Chaco-Anasazi country which experienced the most remarkable growth during the next five or six centuries. Pithouse villages grew to as many as fifty houses in places like Skunk Springs at the base of the Chuska Mountains. The most impressive of these Basketmaker farming districts were located on good farmland, adjacent to mountain areas offering large game, pinon, and spring snow melts to ensure water for germination of seed corn.

In the Southwest, elevation largely determines local climatic conditions. The Pajarito Plateau may have been too high, with too short a growing season, to produce large crops during this time. It likely took many centuries to adapt corn, beans and squash, first brought from Mexico, to the cold upland regions of northern New Mexico.

There is another possibility—an intriguing one which can yet be neither proven or disproven. The Pajarito Plateau, along with a large triangle of mountainous northern New Mexico, may have been inhabited by local populations who clung to the hunting-gathering way of life long after the San Juan Basin had come to rely on corn, beans, and squashes. The clues are tantalizing: little exchange of pottery; no far-flung trade; large, "unsettled" areas of land with no permanent villages separating people with common heritage.

Throughout this triangle, pottery is quite rare until the very end of the early developmental period (about A.D. 800-900). Virtually none of the first finely decorated Anasazi Black-on-white pottery from the late sixth through eighth centuries A.D. has been found in these highlands. Is it conceivable that in all those centuries not one person came to the Polvadera and Obsidian Ridge quarries bearing a painted bowl as an offering in return for the obsidian? One has but to trek to the shrine of the Stone Lions (and see the offerings left by Native Americans—antlers, pottery shards from hundreds of miles away, and an occasional arrowhead) to be truly puzzled. Possibly these forested regions were inhabited by "highlanders" unfriendly to the Anasazi farmers of the surrounding basin-lands.

There is also the odd case of the Rosa Phase pithouses carved into grassy knolls in the Gallina highlands (between Cuba and Lindrith, New Mexico) in the seventh through tenth centuries A.D. These large, deep pithouses, often a dozen to a narrow meadow, and the artifacts found in them share virtually none of the distinguishing characteristics that archeologists identify with the early Chaco-Anasazi. These part-time farmers hunted the west flanks of the Jemez and made their own distinctive pottery. They probably did not engage in external trade, since almost no early Chacoan pottery is found in their villages, and none of theirs is found in early Chacoan ones.

Then, too, there is a wide, desolate "no-man's land" lacking permanent villages of any kind. This separates the Rosa villages from the northeastern frontier of Chacoan development— a frontier never truly settled. Even at the zenith of Chacoan power in the late eleventh century A.D. this area contained only ephemeral, scattered campsites. For these reasons, some archeologists see the Pajarito inhabitants as the southern tip of a great wedge of local mountain peoples who did not participate in Chaco-Anasazi development during the early Christian era.

There is some question as to whether these mountain folk were Anasazi at all. Studies of skeletal remains, some done a half century ago, suggest that the mountains of northern New Mexico were a biological as well as a cultural barrier. The scanty data currently available prevent a definite answer, but the key may be hidden in the unexplored lands of Bandelier and the adjacent canyons.

The Basketmaker period showed significant social and technological developments throughout the Chaco-Anasazi country. Pithouses decreased in size and their internal layout passed beyond the experimental stage to become standardized. Storage cists grew larger, until ones lined with stone slabs were erected above-ground, outside the pithouses. Outdoor ramadas (leans-tos) and cooking areas were common and some villages had modest plazas. In most of the bigger villages, one or more large earth lodges were built. Archeologists believe that these were the first kivas, predecessors of the circular ceremonial chambers dug into Tyuonyi's great plaza nearly eight centuries later.

The dominant, more densely settled villages generally contained much larger quantities of various fine, painted pottery wares than did their poorer neighbors. Precious ornaments and exotic trade goods became more common. Spondylus shell was imported from the Sea of Cortez, a thousand miles to the southwest, then ground into strands of the disc-like beads now called heishi. (Fine heishi is still made by New Mexico's Pueblo Indians and prized by Indian, Hispanic and Anglo buyers. Hundreds of rough shell chips are drilled, then strung onto long strands. Traditionally, these were then tediously hand rolled between two rough sandstone slabs and ground into exquisitely delicate beads.) Turquoise, mined near the present-day village of Cerrillos, was traded west into the Chaco heartland. (Cerrillos turquoise, often a distinctive blue-green color, is still mined by hand from the same deposits.) Small ornamental pendants were fashioned of coral, jet, freshwater shells from Texas, or pipestone from Nebraska, all of which found their way to the Southwest.

With larger plants, ears, and kernels, corn produced larger, more consistent yields. Farming implements were evolving; hafted stone or antler hoes were more sophisticated. Garden plots were more carefully laid out, sometimes with low rock walls to slow runoff, so that more precious rainwater was absorbed by the thin desert soils. Gone were

Woven yucca sandals. Photo by Wyatt Davis, 1940. Courtesy of Museum of New Mexico, negative number 43934.

Thermally efficient Turkey feather blanket used in one form or another for over 1000 years. Blair Clark, photographer, courtesy of Museum of New Mexico, catalog number 46043/11, 1989.

White Mound/La Plata Black on White bowl from late Basketmaker period in northern New Mexico. Photo courtesy of Mike Marshall, Maxwell Museum Collections.

the pill-shaped grinding stones. Larger, more elaborate manos (hand pieces) and trough-shaped metates (grinding stones) were used to grind corn and wild seeds into meal.

By the end of the Basketmaker period, true pithouse villages dotted the bare, windy mesas of the San Juan Basin. Social, religious, and economic life had become more complex. Though intricate woven goods (primarily yucca-fiber sandals and unusual cloaks of turkey feathers and strips of rabbit fur) were still produced, a half-dozen varieties of finely painted, black-on-white ceramic bowls and mugs were being traded across the area. Well-made, neck-banded *ollas*, or pots, for cooking and carrying water were produced locally in nearly every village, and some large, particularly fine plainware ones were also traded over significant distances.

The area around Bandelier continued to lag behind in these developments, and the few surrounding, local settlements were small and scattered. But the Basketmaker folk of the Chaco country had set irreversible forces in motion by the tenth century—forces which were to fundamentally transform prehistoric Southwestern society.

Boomtowns in Basin-Lands
The Chacoan Period

The era of old pithouse villages ended in a whirlwind of change. During the nearly four centuries of Basketmaker development, the number of settlements in the San Juan Basin had increased tenfold. At the very beginning of the Basketmaker period (about A.D. 400), villages hugged the mountains. By the end of the era (about A.D. 800), more than a thousand settlements were scattered across the San Juan Basin, using virtually all the sites having rich soil and dependable water.

Population began to expand rapidly between the ninth and tenth centuries, and there were several new styles of village construction. The first, called Pueblo I, were pithouses flanked by small blocks of masonry or jacal storage rooms. (Jacal is an efficient wattle-and-daub construction technique.) Then, small rectangular houseblocks of masonry rooms appeared, along with a distinctive new, mineral-painted (with iron oxides) Black-on-white ceramic ware named after the Red Mesa Valley near Gallup. By A.D. 950, Red Mesa Black-on-white pottery had spread across the San Juan Basin and into the Bandelier/Santa Fe district. A particularly vibrant wave of economic activity carried trade in these ceramics as far north as Taos and as far east as the Watrous Valley.

The rapid pace of change created an extraordinarily complex archeological record. In many of the upland areas encircling the San Juan Basin, Red Mesa Black-on-white bowls were traded into settlements where pithouses continued to be built. But in the lowlands of the Red Mesa valley itself, pithouse construction ceased. There, eight-to twenty-room masonry pueblos were erected in a virtual

Red Mesa Black-on-white pot. Hallmark pottery of the early Chaco period, A.D. 800s-900s. Photo courtesy of Mike Marshall, Maxwell Museum Collections.

frenzy of construction. At many of the best watered locations, pueblos were built directly on top of old pithouse villages; in some, construction of nearly complete pithouses was halted, gaping holes filled in, and masonry rooms built over the top.

Some remaining pithouses continued in use for a generation or two, then were abandoned. Others were remodeled into kivas, becoming more distinctive (and probably more sacred) as ordinary pithouses disappeared altogether from the 15,000 square miles of drier basin-lands. It was no longer important to locate villages right against the mountains in order to have access to hunting. The focus of economic activity shifted to drier, scrubby basin-lands and, for more

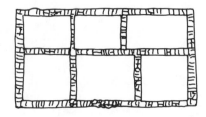

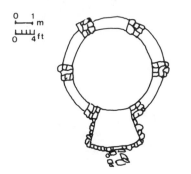

Red Mesa type house block. A small, rectangular or "L"-shaped sandstone pueblo is often found adjacent to a pit-house/"kiva" in the A.D. 800s and 900s. This was a period of explosive growth which followed Basketmaker pithouses and set the stage for the later Chaco Phenomenon. From *Prehistory of the Southwest* by Linda Cordell 1984. Courtesy of Academic Press Inc.

than two centuries, daily survival depended heavily on large-cobbed corn and small game animals.

Archeologists call this the early Pueblo II Period. Rainfall, though not particularly abundant, was relatively stable from year to year. This predictability allowed the Chaco-Anasazi to expand into previously unused countryside. By A.D. 1000, many small pueblos had been built where no pit-house village had ever existed. Many Chaco-Anasazi farmers had begun to pioneer dry-farming techniques in less protected basin settings, while others pushed eastward toward the Rio Grande.

Just after A.D. 1000, farmsteads covered all but a rough arc along the northwestern edge of the San Juan Basin.

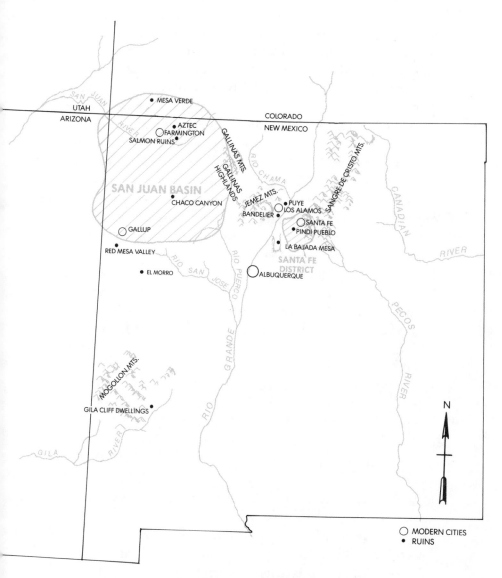

Late Chacoan and Upland sites.

Corn, several varieties of pre-modern "pinto" beans, squash, melons, pigweed and native grasses (such as Indian Rice Grass) made up most of the diet. Meat was obtained primarily from rabbits, domesticated turkeys, even kangaroo rats and gophers. Large game was quite scarce, though occasional bighorn sheep, prong-horn antelope, and deer were taken.

At Bandelier, obsidian was still quarried and made into darts or true arrowheads, later found by archeologists in ancient settlements along the Rio Grande. At some of these farmsteads, local inhabitants continued to build pithouses—an anomaly which has caused archeologists to use a different approach to Rio Grande archeology. Between Española and Albuquerque, both pithouse villages and small masonry or adobe pueblos contain traces of the Chacoan pottery, and many more bones of large animals are found than in the western Chaco country. Microscopic pollens from corn and other garden crops are also found in soil samples taken at these sites.

Bandelier's strong economic connections were with the local lowlands. Local trade seems to have connected villages north to south along the Rio Grande, for even at this late date (A.D. 1000) decorated Mogollon pottery continued to be found mixed in with locally-made cooking wares. But by A.D. 1050 Chacoan society had become an unprecedented force in the prehistoric Southwest. Enormous expansion took place at the large, old settlements in Chaco Canyon, on the slopes of Mount Taylor, near Gallup, and along the lower Chaco River to the northwest of Chaco Canyon.

Some Chacoan settlements even grew into huge district trading villages, now called "outliers," and ancient foot paths were expanded into carefully finished roadways. The oldest villages—favored for natural growth by their good soil and water—almost always have older pithouse villages beneath them. One of these is the magnificent Pueblo Bonito at Chaco Canyon National Monument. Others of the great Chacoan "towns" had not yet been built. The great kiva at Aztec Ruins National Monument, Cliff House at Mesa Verde, Tyuonyi here at Bandelier, and Atsinna Pueblo at El Morro were all built after Chacoan society had peaked in size.

The radical change in the quality and complexity of Anasazi development after A.D. 1050 has caused most contemporary archeologists to consider the late Chacoan period as a separate entity. However, many books on Southwestern archeology remain outdated, and thus confuse the casual reader by grouping Chacoan society with the large ruins of Mesa Verde, Bandelier, and Montezuma's Castle and calling all of these the "Great Pueblo," or Pueblo III Period (A.D. 1100-1300). While all of these ruins are "Great Pueblos" in a descriptive sense, they belong together only in the sense that one gave rise indirectly to the other, mostly through a series of unplanned events.

Mesa Verde and Bandelier are separated from Chaco society by a century or more in time and, unlike Chaco, are *all* in forested uplands. The final, and fabulous, "Chaco Phenomenon" is best considered the very zenith of Pueblo II society—found primarily in the lower, drier basin-lands of western and central New Mexico. The immense sandstone structures created during this zenith, at Chaco Canyon, Aztec Ruins, and Salmon Ruins (not a national monument) near Bloomfield, New Mexico, belong together; they are all in the San Juan Basin and they were erected in about a two-hundred-year time span.

In *late* Chacoan times remarkable social, economic, architectural, and technological complexity replaced the raw geographic expansion of earlier boom years. By A.D. 1100, the Chaco-Anasazi were spread over more than thirty-

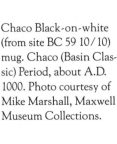

Chaco Black-on-white (from site BC 59 10/10) mug. Chaco (Basin Classic) Period, about A.D. 1000. Photo courtesy of Mike Marshall, Maxwell Museum Collections.

thousand square miles, an area nearly the size of Scotland. The number of villages had again increased nearly ten-fold over the late Basketmaker period. Ten thousand Chaco-Anasazi farmsteads and trading villages and nearly one hundred major "outlier" towns were linked in a trade/food/transportation/ceremonial network.

Small margins of surplus corn from thousands of modest farmsteads were needed to fuel the infrastructure necessary to incorporate diverse peoples and diverse local trading districts into a functional whole. But Chacoan society had outgrown its agricultural underpinnings at a time when the need for efficient food distribution was expanding. The Red Mesa Valley, one of its early "breadbaskets," already had languished as the thin soils were depleted after two centuries of constant harvesting. The large, scattered populations suffered from inefficiencies in transportation and local food shortages, especially villages that no longer produced their own food—only pottery for trade. Probably some people had no fertile land of their own to work, and reports from those who had pioneered farmsteads on the eastern frontier (the valley of the Pecos) two generations before were not glowing. Expansion into New Mexico's drier eastern plains brought new hardships and confrontation with hostile plainsmen.

By studying burial sites and associated human skeletons archeologists know that the economy became increasingly fragile in late Chacoan times. One study estimated that infant mortality was nearly fifty percent in the Gallup region by A.D. 1000. (By contrast, when two percent of the infants in any American locality die before one year of age, it is considered a public health crisis.) Human bones recovered from other small Chacoan farmsteads also show consistent evidence of malnutrition.

Chacoan society—like our own—was enormously successful, but had its problems. Also like modern America, Chacoan society was probably an amalgamation of different ethnic and language groups. Because different basic units of measurement were used within some buildings at Chaco Canyon, archeologists speculate that there are adjacent masonry room-blocks which were constructed by crews from separate ethnic groups.

In the late eleventh century, these problems pushed the Chacoans into building wider, more elaborate roadways. About the same time, skilled masons built huge new villages, such as Pueblo Pintado on Chaco Canyon's new East Road to its desolate north-eastern frontier. This frontier was shared with the Gallina villagers who earlier had built the Rosa pithouses. An immense pile of sandstone enclosing sixty huge rooms, from foundation to the lofty ponderosa

Pueblo Pintado ruins east of Chaco Canyon. Built in A.D. 1060-61.
Photo courtesy of Museum of New Mexico, negative number 80739.

rafters Pueblo Pintado was built entirely in the winter of
A.D. 1060-61—quite like one magnificent "WPA-style" pro-
ject right out of the Roosevelt era. No ancient village had
existed there previously, so there were no settlers to serve
administratively and no nearby farmsteads requiring a district granary. By the early twelfth century, Salmon Ruin and
Aztec Ruin had been built and incorporated into the Chacoan economic sphere, and other centers in Chaco Canyon
were being enlarged. Lower elevations at Bandelier, in the
Cochiti Reservoir area, near Santa Fe, and in the Galisteo
Basin were populated and, at least tenuously, incorporated
into Chacoan trade networks. For a time, Chacoan society
had cleverly converted the traditional hand-tool horticul-
ture of an ungenerous, sometimes capricious, semi-arid climate into a political and economic power more impressive

than most feudal princes could even contemplate.

But with grandeur came both rigidity and fragility. Chronic problems mounted. Even as the last great building episodes were taking place at Chaco Canyon, small farmsteads in the outlying districts were being abandoned by the hundreds. Field archeologists familiar with the San Juan Basin have noted that the complex late pottery styles, such as the Chaco-McElmo Black-on-white bowls found at Pueblo Alto, Chetro Ketl and other large towns in Chaco Canyon, have never been found at the small farmsteads in the central basin, for the inhabitants were already gone.

As the small farming pueblos were abandoned, new ones were being built—most in higher elevations near the edges of the San Juan Basin. The movement started slowly, then rushed toward a peak about A.D. 1140. Ironically, the very farmers and villagers necessary to sustain Chacoan society had "voted with their feet" and moved to the higher mesas around the margins of the San Juan Basin. By midcentury, the fabric of Chacoan society ceased to exist. It was the end of another chapter for the Anasazi.

Changing seasons of rainfall, bad crop years, scarce firewood, droughts, disease, malnutrition, and conflict with "outsiders" have all been advanced as causes for the Chacoan decline. In truth, many things join together to bring a great society to its knees, and so it probably was with the Chaco-Anasazi. Exit the Chaco-Anasazi of western basin-lands; enter the Mesa Verde, Rio Grande, and Little Colorado Anasazi of the high mesas and cool ponderosa country. In and around Bandelier National Monument the end of Chacoan society was played out and the beginnings of a new society, the Rio Grande Anasazi, was formed during the tumultuous two centuries following Chaco Canyon's decline.

Aerial photo of ruins at El Moro National Monument east of Zuni Pueblo. This great, natural reservoir atop a stunning, rocky promontory first drew permanent settlers to it during the upland period. Those who built there only endured a few generations before abandoning their pueblo, called Atsinna. Photo courtesy of Baker Aero Works—Tom Baker, 1989.

Aerial photo of Pueblo Alto with traces of ancient roads converging at upper left. Photo courtesy of Baker Aero Works—Tom Baker, 1989.

Facing page, left: San Clemente Glaze "A" polychrome pot. Early Riverine Period (A.D. 1300s). Photo courtesy of Mike Marshall, Maxwell Museum Collections.

Facing page, right: Sankawe Black on Cream pot—a distinctive style produced on the Pajarito Plateau during the late Riverine Period (A.D. 1500-1650). Photo courtesy of Mike Marshall, Maxwell Museum Collections.

Aerial photo of Pueblo Colorado as the foot of a cliff in the
Galisteo Basin. Photo courtesy of Baker Aero Works—Tom Baker,
1989.

country from southern Colorado to central New Mexico receives more summer thunderstorms than any other place in the United States. This is due to seasonal air masses and has been a pattern since prehistoric times. After Chacoan decline, Anasazi society literally moved uphill to unite with the mountain thunders.

The practical implications of living at one elevation or another are still with us today. Albuquerque, 5100 feet above sea level, receives an average of only eight inches of rainfall per year. Santa Fe, at an elevation of 7000 feet on the drier west slope of the Sangre de Cristo Mountains, receives an average of thirteen inches, while Los Alamos at 7300 feet on the wetter, east-facing Pajarito receives about twenty inches per year. More abundant moisture notwithstanding, any resident of Los Alamos can tell you just how hard it is to raise a crop of tall, large-cobbed corn in a backyard garden. The same variety of corn will generally produce successively smaller ears from Albuquerque to Santa Fe to Los Alamos.

It was much the same in prehistoric times. Corn cobs recovered from ruins of the A.D. 1100s in the higher elevations around Bandelier National Monument are invariably small compared to those recovered from earlier Chacoan sites of the San Juan Basin. And the "pueblo corn," grown three centuries later in the huge Classic Period Pueblos along the Rio Grande in the part of Bandelier Monument now submerged under Cochiti Reservoir, was much larger.

Archeologists have long been puzzled by corn of the Upland Period found in ancient caches around Bandelier, pronouncing it "retrogressive" or "primitive." Some may have been, since local cross-breeding quickly introduces genetic variation in corn; but most was, like disappointingly small modern corn from local gardens, simply stunted by cool nighttime temperatures. The mass of population, which characterized the Chaco-Anasazi era, simply could not all be supported on the reduced crop yields imposed by the highlands. Hunting again became as important as farming. Some people starved; others raided. Given a large population and the ecological limitations of farming in the mountain districts, it should not be a surprise that the twelfth century was exceedingly difficult.

Previously, the Chacoan trade network had softened the hard edge of local scarcity. More than a dozen varieties of elaborate, painted pottery were regularly traded between hundreds of well-built villages. The labor invested in creating prized pottery could buy corn, and district granaries could at least provide secure supplies of seed corn in poor years. But the Chacoan economic network was already rapidly disintegrating. This pushed even more impoverished families of common farmers high into the Pajarito Plateau. The first to arrive in Bandelier did not even build pueblos; they reverted to excavating deep pithouses in hidden coves, and locally-made pottery was supplemented only occasionally by one or two trade-wares. So, Pajarito sites of the early 1100s rarely have much fine pottery.

Many archeologists at first found it hard to believe that progress and evolution in architectural styles had "run backwards" after the Chaco decline, again producing pithouses after more than two centuries of pueblo architecture in the Anasazi world. This phenomenon is not really so surprising; nearly eight hundred years after dugout-pithouses were built high on the Pajarito Plateau, Anglo-American homesteaders in eastern New Mexico, Texas, and Oklahoma were also building sod "dugouts" to live in until the first few crops had been planted and harvested. Only later did such "sod-busters" build the neat frame homes, courthouses, and churches considered typical of Midwestern Anglo-American society.

These first settlements of deep pithouses were tucked

away in the higher elevations of the Pajarito, and in many other mountainous areas across the Four Corners country. Archeologists generally detest the very idea of such sites, which they completely ruin neat developmental charts in textbooks. They are often characterized as "atypical," "isolated kivas," "misdated," or "contaminated" by pottery manufactured long after the pithouse itself was dug. But they are there, nonetheless—silent testimony to several generations of difficult adaptation to life in the uplands. On the Pajarito, Anasazi farmers made out as best they could without the benefits of Chacoan economic and political power.

Within a generation, by A.D. 1160-1190, styles of architecture had become more "normal," and small masonry pueblos were again being built, this time in the highlands. Those in Bandelier are usually at slightly lower elevations than many of the earlier pithouses, but more than one was built right atop a pithouse. New forms of black-on-white pottery characterize this period. Instead of crushing iron ores to create black pigments as was done with the earlier Chacoan pottery, potters began to use various organic (plant) pigments to create bold black-on-white designs.

For most archeologists, the appearance of organic-painted pottery in small masonry pueblos of six to thirty-six rooms marks the real beginning of the Coalition Period (traditionally dated A.D. 1200-1325, but herein about 1160-1290). The organic paint technique is usually described as having moved from Arizona (Kayenta Anasazi) to the Mesa Verde country, thence to the Rio Grande. But, some archeologists believe it is more accurate to associate the rise of organic-painted pottery manufacture in the highlands of the Southwest with the simultaneous decline of Chacoan society in the lower elevations.

Santa Fe Black-on-white bowl, upland period. Note simple design and "ghostly" quality of dark grey carbon paint. Blair Clark photographer. Courtesy of Museum of New Mexico, catalog number 43341/11, 1989.

In Bandelier, the most easily identified organic pottery of the period is called Santa Fe Black-on-white. In fact, this pottery has bold but ghostly off-black designs over a gray background. Hundreds of small masonry pueblos built on the Pajarito Plateau during the late 1100s contain this pottery, but very few have ever been excavated. These sites generate little interest among either scholars or the public, for they are not visually spectacular. Most were inhabited only for a generation or two, so they yield few museum specimens and little accurately datable material.

In fact, data from excavations at major ruins and from archeological field surveys often yield very different pictures of what happened in prehistoric times, so it is not safe to recreate the past based on only one or the other. Nearly all of Bandelier's several dozen excavated sites were founded after the late A.D. 1200s, but an intensive archeological survey conducted on adjacent lands between 1977 and 1980

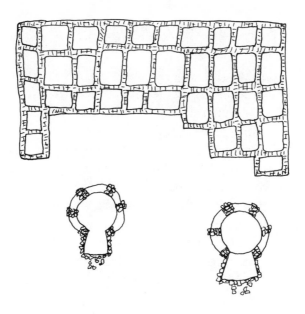

Drawing of typical house block of a Coalition Period Pueblo. After *El Palacio*, vol. 62, nos. 5 and 6.

turned up another 880 sites. About fifty-five percent of these were actually Coalition Period, while just under thirty percent were of the Rio Grande Classic Period (A.D. 1325-1600). Yet virtually all of the literature written on Bandelier National Monument covers only the Rio Grande Classic Period. Some scholars even portray Bandelier as inhabited for about three centuries (A.D. 1300 to 1600), although the most intensive habitation actually spanned the period from about A.D. 1160-1290.

The Monument area was highly utilized compared to other parts of the ancient Southwest. An analysis of archeological projects conducted throughout the Chaco-Anasazi country after 1960 indicates an average of just over twelve sites per square mile in large districts which trained archeological teams painstakingly walked foot-by-foot. However, a UCLA survey of lands adjacent to Bandelier found that about *twenty* prehistoric sites per square mile were built on the Pajarito, nearly double the average.

A more recent survey conducted by the National Park Service in Bandelier itself found 470 new archeological sites in only 3,356 acres of mesa land adjacent to the middle elevations in Frijoles Canyon. That computes to a staggering *ninety sites* per square mile! Only the greatest Chaco-Anasazi outliers with their nearby farmsteads and a few late Rio Grande Classic Pueblos show similar intensity of use anywhere in the eastern Anasazi world. It may be that this figure cannot be accurately projected onto unsurveyed areas in the Monument, for Frijoles Canyon carries twice as much water (a critical factor in farming) as any other canyon in Bandelier Monument.

By roughly A.D. 1190, the majority of the small Santa Fe Black-on-white masonry pueblos had been built. Unlike later villages, many of these did not have kivas. These sites are most numerous north of the Monument near well-watered canyons like Guaje and Bayo, but one good example in the Monument is "House Across the Way" near the mouth of Lummis Canyon at only 5400 feet elevation. This eight-room pueblo, like others of its period, had more kinds of pottery than the rare, early pithouses, but most cooking ware was still locally made. Exotic trade goods—semiprecious stone, shells, or feathers—are seldom found in sites of this time period.

Then, about A.D. 1200, Anasazi clans began to build cliff-palaces. Though tree-ring dates of A.D. 1300-1400 are generally given for the cliff ruins, like "Long House" and "Snake Village" in Frijoles Canyon, these datable beam samples were taken many decades after the original excavations conducted by Edgar Lee Hewett in the early twentieth century. Most were retrieved as discarded beam fragments, often charred, in "back-dirt" piled up from excavations then long completed. The precise placement, or "provenience," of these timbers prior to excavation is usually in doubt. As a consequence, none of the sites near the Visitor's Center has been dated with precision. In fact, the major construction at most of the larger cliff-dwellings found throughout the Southwest took place from roughly A.D. 1200 to A.D. 1260, and the oldest pottery found in the talus slopes below Long House and Talus House at Bandelier are broadly dated to this period.

Cliff-houses are both utilitarian and magnificent to behold. They are generally in good defensive locations and hard to attack, a characteristic of many sites built between A.D. 1200 and 1260 throughout the Southwest. Quite energy efficient, they act as huge solar collectors to absorb the sun's winter rays, yet are cool in summer because most are protected from summer sun by rock overhangs. Virtually every Southwestern cliff-dwelling faces south, southeast, or southwest. *None* face north! At Bandelier all of the fascinating cliff-dwellings and cave-rooms are found on the north side of Frijoles Creek. Not one is to be found in the soft rock of the canyon's south cliff—which faces north. In winter, deep snow often lingers for weeks on that empty cliff face, while sunlit entrances of snow-free rooms line the north wall of the canyon.

Many archeologists propose that the higher, isolated cave (called cavate) rooms above Frijoles Canyon and Otowi were winter retreats for families. It is quite likely they were, for there were not enough good cliff faces to support every large pueblo. Also many mountain canyons in the Southwest are subject to brutal "wind tunnel" effects when cold winds rush through each evening or during winter storms. Tijeras Canyon, through which Interstate Highway 25 passes east of Albuquerque, is one locally well known wind tunnel. No prehistoric dwellings at all are found against exposed portions of its south-facing wall.

South facing cliff wall within Frijoles Canyon, Bandelier National
Monument. Photo by Mary Powell, 1989.

North facing cliff wall on the opposite side of Frijoles Canyon from
the photo on facing page. Note the lack of cave rooms and ruins on
the north side. Photo by Mary Powell, 1989.

Gila National Monument. Photo by O.C. Hinman. Courtesy of
Museum of New Mexico, negative number 6205.

Cliff-houses were not the major form of Anasazi
architecture during these centuries but were one of several
types used. Within a few miles of most major cliff dwellings
there are probably a hundred or more contemporaneous
ordinary pueblos. Many of these can be found on the flat
mesa-tops above cave-rooms, strung out along the canyons
which cross-cut the Pajarito Plateau. Others were built in
the canyon bottoms. The period between A.D. 1200 and
1290 brought other changes to Bandelier, many of which
are just now being investigated.

At national monuments, emphasis is placed on preservation, so very little excavation has been done using modern scientific methods either in Bandelier or in nearby
areas. The great period of excavation throughout the Pajarito Plateau was before World War II. In Frijoles Canyon
itself, most excavations were actually completed before
World War I, so there are no major, modern excavation

63

reports to consult for the immediate area. However, several quite recent excavation reports are available for the lower canyon mouths near, or in, Cochiti Reservoir. These are invaluable, but the archeology of the lower elevations along the Rio Grande is somewhat different.

So, using survey results, modest "test" excavations, and the reports from lower elevations along the Rio Grande, archeologists have pieced together a general picture of the thirteenth century in the Bandelier area. There may have been a number of unusually severe winters in the early A.D. 1200s, for along with cliff-houses, thermally efficient pit-houses were once again being built. Such pithouses, found near Taos, the Gallina area, in Bandelier, and in central New Mexico, have an average date of A.D. 1223. As with the highland pithouses of a century earlier, many archeologists will reserve judgement on just what these can tell us until more are found, excavated, and dated by laboratory methods. These later pithouses all have some striking characteristics in common: they are found primarily in moderate elevations of about 6500 feet; they average about 2 feet in depth; and they often have surprising quantities of well-made tradeware pottery in them. These are not kivas. From the ground-surface, they look no different, but when excavated, they typically have hearths without any of the special architectural features unique to the true sacred chambers.

The most common trade pottery found in these small pithouse settlements is St. John's Polychrome or its variants. This pottery, traded into mountainous areas near Albu-querque, Bandelier, and Mesa Verde, was manufactured either somewhere in the uplands of east-central Arizona or near the Zuni region, about 250 miles southwest of the Monument. The presence of trade-wares from distant locali-ties is quite significant for it tells archeologists that a high-

St. John's Polychrome bowl. Hallmark of the late Upland Period. About A.D. 1175-1275. Photo courtesy of Mike Marshall, Maxwell Museum Collections.

land trading network had replaced the old Chacoan trading patterns after nearly a half century of interruption. It is even possible that the pithouse dwellers were distinct clans, new-comers or traders from elsewhere in New Mexico. No one currently knows why they did not live in the contemporaneous cliff houses.

So, just after A.D. 1200, cliff-houses, small pueblos with kivas, and pithouses could all be found within a few miles of one another; but many of the smaller masonry pueblos were soon abandoned. New pueblos were again being established in the lowlands near Cochiti Reservoir. Kiva House is a good example. It contained twenty-one rooms and three kivas, and a dozen styles of painted pottery were found. In contrast to House Across the Way, it was built just after A.D. 1200, was approximately twice as large, had kivas, and contained pottery traded in from the Zuni, Socorro, and El Morro areas. In contrast to the small Santa Fe Black-on-

65

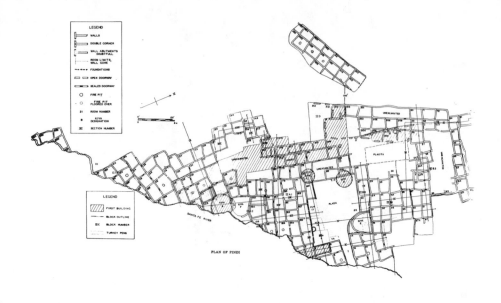

Site plan of Pindi Pueblo (LA1) near Santa Fe. From *The Excavation of Pindi Pueblo*, by Stanley A. Stubbs and W.S. Stallings, Jr.

white sites of the Pajarito's higher mesas, it was renovated for reuse during the later Classic Period.

A similar and more famous site, Pindi Pueblo, near Santa Fe, was founded at this time. Immortalized as *LA 1* (Laboratory of Anthropology site number one), Pindi Pueblo was the very first site formally numbered into the great New Mexico Laboratory of Anthropology's serial site file, which now includes records of nearly seventy thousand ruins. Kiva House, Pindi Pueblo, and Colina Verde in the Galisteo Basin are proof that at about A.D. 1200 the Anasazi world had tentatively begun to look downhill from its lofty, remote mountain tops. But most of those lowland settlements were rather quickly abandoned and the Anasazi did not rebuild them until a century later. The highland settlements continued to flourish.

In the third decade of the A.D. 1200s, huge mesa-top

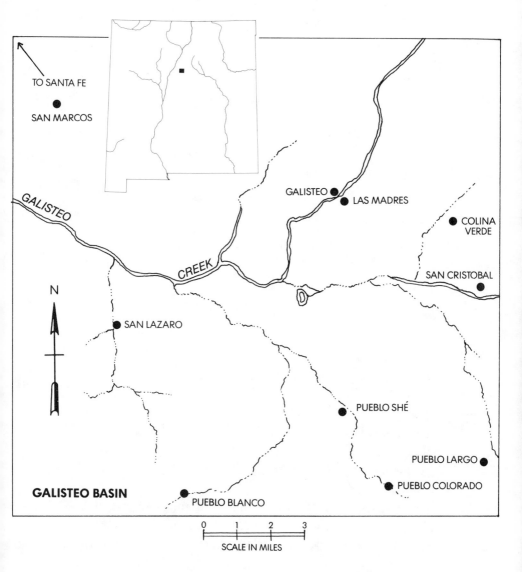

TO SANTA FE

● SAN MARCOS

GALISTEO

CREEK

GALISTEO ● ● LAS MADRES

● COLINA
VERDE

● SAN CRISTOBAL

N

● SAN LAZARO

● PUEBLO SHÉ

PUEBLO LARGO ●

GALISTEO BASIN

● PUEBLO COLORADO

● PUEBLO BLANCO

| 0 | 1 | 2 | 3 |

SCALE IN MILES

These large villages of the Galisteo are typical of the Rio Grande
classic, or Riverine, Period A.D. 1315-1650.

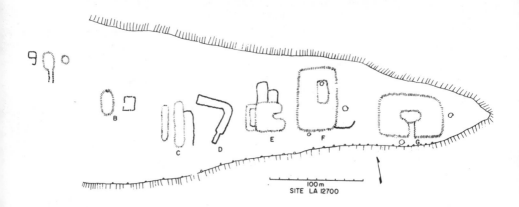

Site plan of LA 12,700, Guaje Canyon Ruin, north of Bandelier National Monument. On file at the Laboratory of Anthropology, Archeological Site Records, Santa Fe, New Mexico. Drawing believed to be by Charlie Steen.

plaza sites were being built throughout the Pajarito and on similar mesas from eastern Arizona north into Colorado. Those found around Bandelier are quite forbidding and mysterious since virtually none have been fully excavated.

Most of these local villages consist of fallen tiers of rooms, built of rough, rectangular blocks hand-carved from the Pajarito's relatively soft volcanic tuff. A "textbook" example of such a site is LA 12700, also known as Guaje Canyon Ruin, about one and a half miles north of Los Alamos. It straddles a narrow, sloping mesa-top on U.S. Forest Service land about 7000 feet above sea level. Its three immense, rectangular roomblocks each enclose a plaza. Remarkably, this plaza site also contains five deep, circular kivas which had been carefully hand-pecked into the mesa's soft bedrock! The Guaje site represents the last full chapter in Bandelier's Upland Period.

Villages such as Guaje Canyon Ruin seem to have been

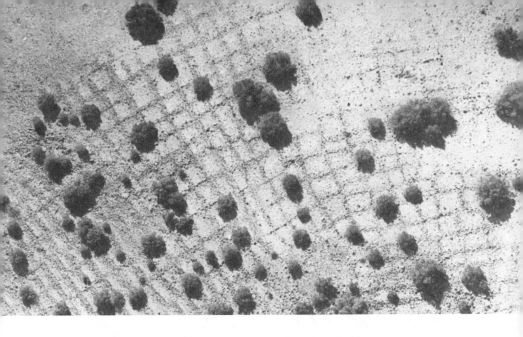

Aerial photo. Grid gardens on east side of Rio Grande. Moisture conserving grid gardens came into use during the A.D. 1200s and were an important feature of Pueblo agriculture for centuries afterwards. Photo courtesy of Baker Aero Works—Tom Baker, 1989.

built between A.D. 1200 and 1270, only to be abandoned within twenty or thirty years. Like the Guaje site, many also have reservoirs built nearby, and some mesa-top areas are neatly gridded-off into small garden plots. Cobble-mulched grid gardens first became widespread in the late A.D. 1200s, probably a response to dry conditions.

These cobble-beds appear to be quite unlikely gardens, but they actually create good conditions for planting crops in areas where natural evaporation rates are high. Each spring, for hundreds of years, farmers of the Pajarito had to hand-carry water to every young plant! During late spring, when seeds must germinate, and tender, young garden plants can be hopelessly scorched by a single bright, dry afternoon under the penetrating sunlight of high altitudes, every drop of moisture retained in the soil is critical. In the area around Bandelier, dark, angular basalt cobbles are sometimes used to mulch these rocky grid-gardens. Mois-

Petroglyphs on rock jutting into pool. This pool of water is in a
small rocky canyon on east side of Rio Grande—a typical setting
for petroglyphs carved in the Rio Grande style after A.D. 1300.
Photo courtesy of Baker Aero Works—Tom Baker, 1989.

Pool in rocky arroyo in the malpias south east of Bandelier on the
east side of the Rio Grande. Such pools often were a source of
water, tediously hand carried to nourish young crops planted on
nearby mesa tops. Photo courtesy of Baker Aero Works—Tom
Baker, 1989.

ture is trapped on the cool underside of the rock where it touches the soil. Underneath, the earth will be cooler and more moist than the thin, dusty gravel just a foot away. One recent "backyard" study in Arizona suggests that, once heated by the afternoon sun, a layer of dark-colored cobbles arranged in a rectangle measuring one yard on a side can actively precipitate several gallons of water daily from the "dry" evening air which blows across the Southwest's mesas!

Other technological innovations came to Bandelier during this period. These included fully-grooved axes, which were far more efficient for chopping roof beams and firewood, and the full-slab sandstone metates (grinding stones) whose larger grinding surfaces speeded up the production of corn meal.

Plaza sites of the late A.D. 1200s were once thought to be mainly north of Bandelier and to have been built by ancestors of today's Tewa-speaking pueblos (San Juan, Santa Clara, San Ildefonso, Nambe, and Tesuque). The more southerly sites, like Tyuonyi, were thought to have been built by ancestors of the eastern Keresan-speaking pueblos (Cochiti, Santo Domingo, San Felipe, Santa Ana, and Zia). But recent field investigations and analysis of aerial photographs suggest that the largest plaza-sites actually tend to be on mesas where rainfall was comparatively abundant and small streams flowed in the canyons below. It happens that there are simply more well-watered canyons to the north of Bandelier than to the south. Geography accounts more for these differences than do the presumed habits of ancestral Tewa as opposed to Keres.

The late A.D. 1200s saw the resurgence of corn agriculture, large-village society, and a well-defined trading network over large parts of the highland Southwest. Located on easily defended mesas, with garden plots both adjacent

Sandstone slab manos and metates, used for grinding corn into meal, from a Chaco Canyon ruin. The large grinding surfaces were very efficient compared to earlier ones. Photo courtesy of the National Park Service, Bandelier National Monument.

to the village and in the canyon bottoms below, such sites exhibit several styles of agriculture, and those with reservoirs could withstand extended siege. On the Pajarito, the largest plaza-sites contain more than four hundred ground-floor rooms, larger than the fabled Pueblo Bonito at Chaco Canyon, but, in contrast, were invariably short-lived. It was not a time of true abundance.

· Scholars disagree on just why the final chapter of the Upland Period proved so fragile. Far to the south, there were recurring droughts throughout the ancient Aztec world; their written records confirm that this "great drought" prevailed between A.D. 1276 and 1299. The presence of mesa-top villages with cobbled gardens and reservoirs over a wide region of the Southwest tends to support the view that

Aerial photo of Puye near Santa Clara Pueblo. This is typical of large mesa-top villages first founded in the mid A.D. 1200s during the Upland Period. Some, like Puye, were later expanded during the Riverine Period when drought or local conflict forced Rio Grande populations into nearby uplands. Such sites typically have "cavate" rooms carved into cliff-faces below the main ruin. Photo courtesy of Baker Aero Works—Tom Baker, 1989.

the great drought worked its hardships at Bandelier too. In contrast, recent UCLA investigations, which also reconstructed local climatic patterns, do not conclude that protracted droughts were a feature of life on the Pajarito in the late A.D. 1200s. Paleo-climatology is not yet an exact science.

Perhaps other facts should be considered. If probable dates of abandonment are plotted (from the most recent pottery found at each) for four hundred or five hundred villages dating to the late A.D. 1200s at Mesa Verde, the El Morro district, in the Gallina highlands, on the Pajarito, and in the Manzano Mountains southeast of Albuquerque, a singular fact emerges: prehistoric farming districts on the drier western slopes of mountain ranges were generally abandoned twenty to thirty years earlier than those on the more moist east-facing land masses. The high mesas at El Morro and Mesa Verde were abandoned before the wooded mesas at Bandelier or the east slopes of the Sandias at Albuquerque, fifty miles to the south.

By A.D. 1290, the late-blossoming Upland Period around Bandelier began to disintegrate rapidly. The large mesa-top plaza-sites fell silent, and population again scattered. Many people started new settlements in nearby "lowlands" around Santa Fe and in the Galisteo Basin, while others settled in the best-watered canyon bottoms. Nearly two centuries had passed since decline set in at Chaco Canyon. Throughout the Upland Period, settlements shifted from one locale to another, and whole villages, perhaps even major language groups, migrated whenever local crops failed several years running.

Almost no villages built during the Upland Period, except for some of the cliff-houses and large pueblos along permanent streams, were inhabited very long. Most were lived in, abandoned, renovated, abandoned again. And, once again, a great trading network collapsed. Thus, the beautiful red-and-black polychrome bowls were no longer available as trade-wares from the Arizona uplands.

Many pueblo peoples experimented with new village locations just at the dawn of the Rio Grande Classic period, but virtually all of those who prospered had settled along permanent streams or rivers. Strangely, even as population declined in the upper elevations at Bandelier, some of its most famous sites (like Tyuonyi) were being founded. But the hardships of the Upland Period and frequent migrations had already erased the archeologically traceable roots of their founders.

Late Classic Puebloan Society
The Riverine Period

About A.D. 1300, a major reconfiguration of Anasazi society again took place. Most archeologists consider the appearance of glaze-painted pottery to be the hallmark of the Rio Grande Classic Period. In fact, there were many more fundamental changes than the mere replacement of carbon painted black-on-white bowls with "Rio Grande" glazed yellow or glaze-on-red ones. The name "Rio Grande Classic" itself confuses many readers who, logically, suppose that only those Anasazi flourished who had located along the Rio Grande. Many did move to the Rio Grande about that time, but there is a broader, more compelling, reality hidden in that move.

In the late A.D. 1200s, Anasazi society reassessed its possibilities, abandoning both high mesas and dry-farming of mesa tops for the more certain agricultural techniques of flood-plain farming and small-scale irrigation. Except in the Hopi mesa country, rivers and dependable creeks throughout the Southwest drew farmers away from the more remote uplands. It is more sensible to think of this as a geographically widespread Riverine Period than only a "Rio Grande" Period.

Although some irrigation was practiced during the heyday of Chaco and Mimbres societies in the eleventh century, it did not become the norm until nearly three hundred years later. In addition, far more elaborate terracing of hillsides was used to prevent erosion and to slow rainwater runoff so that it penetrated the soil. Grid-gardens grew in size and complexity. La Bajada Mesa, just southeast of Bandelier, had huge areas of neatly gridded garden plots which can still be seen clearly from aerial photographs. True irrigation canals were also built. Many of the Pajarito's springs

75

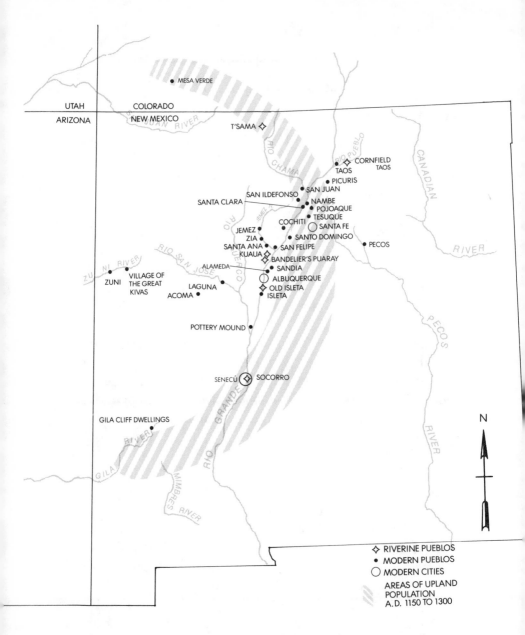

The Modern Pueblos and important ruins of the Riverine Period.

and streams were diverted into small, but effective, stone-lined aqueducts, and elaborate irrigation systems were built up over the centuries. Some historians think of the irrigation ditches, or *acequias*, as a purely Spanish innovation, but archeologists know that is not the case.

With the change in style of agriculture came another wave of "migrations" into or out of local districts. Traditional territories again overlapped, just as they had after the Chacoan decline, leaving the geographic distribution of important language groups an even more complicated mosaic than before. The upland areas around Mesa Verde, El Morro, and Gila Cliff Dwellings National Monuments were largely abandoned. The Riverine Period in Bandelier, as elsewhere, involved a systematic trek down to the permanent creeks and rivers.

In Bandelier, on high mesas several miles west of the Visitor's Center, there are small Upland Period masonry pueblos of the late A.D. 1100s. Downhill are the large mesa-top plaza villages of the late (A.D. 1200s) Upland Period. In Frijoles Canyon itself lies Tyuonyi, which was founded just as the Upland Period was evolving into the Riverine. Each downstream site is a bit newer than the last until Frijoles Creek runs into the Rio Grande. There at its confluence are the villages of the local Rio Grande Classic Period. Along the Rio Grande there are a number of "multicomponent" sites, which have been used during two or more distinct time periods. Since the uphill march began in late Chacoan times, lowland sites which date to about A.D. 1100 will often have a Classic Period "component" built over the over the top. Most of these can be dated to A.D. 1350 or 1400. The long and arduous "round-trip" into the high country and back again took three centuries.

Hidden in the confusion of the early fourteenth century, there were also some fascinating regularities. The earli-

Aerial photo of the huge Sapawi site on El Rito Creek (Chama Valley). A modern football field would easily fit into the plaza of this immense, adobe pueblo of the Riverine Period. Population seasonally flowed out of such villages as agriculturalists took up temporary residence in modest, isolated "fieldhouses" scattered across many square miles of adjacent farmland. Photo courtesy of Baker Aero Works— Tom Baker, 1989.

est Riverine pueblos were modest in size and located on easily fortified hillsides above rivers like the Chama or Rio Grande. Puebloan peoples generally moved south out of Colorado, following major streams as corridors for relocating their settlements. At the same time, Mogollon peoples of the Gila National Forest moved either down stream along the Gila River (southeast into Arizona) or northward along the Rio Grande toward Albuquerque. The Indian population of New Mexico probably was halved by the two centuries of hardship following Chacoan decline, but Riverine farmers invariably maintained access to nearby mountain districts for hunting territories. The net result of these changes was that by the early A.D. 1300s, there were dense farming populations along northern New Mexico's rivers, from the Chama Valley south to the area around Socorro. Bandelier figures prominently in this geographical redistribution, for the Pajarito Plateau was a major frontier area.

Aerial photo of Poshu in the Chama Valley. Note modern houses for
scale. This site is typical of the northern "Biscuitware" sites which
were contemporaneous with the southern Pajarito villages producing
Rio Grande glazewares of the Riverine Period. Photo courtesy of
Baker Aero Works—Tom Baker, 1989.

Biscuit A. Riverine Period bowl, about A.D. 1350-1450, from northern Rio Grande. Photo courtesy of Mike Marshall, Maxwell Museum Collections.

Biscuit B. Riverine Period (A.D. 1400-1550) pot from northern Rio Grande. Photo courtesy of Mike Marshall, Maxwell Museum Collections.

Chupardero Black-on-white bowls were first manufactured in the late upland period, but endured for several centuries afterwards. They were traded widely throughout central New Mexico's uplands. Courtesy of the Museum of New Mexico, catalog Number 46345/11, 1989.

From the Pajarito north, the Rio Grande glazes never did replace the Black-on-white pottery styles of earlier centuries. New Black-on-whites, which were to endure for several centuries, were created. Around Bandelier, Biscuit ware, a thick, Black-on-white pottery made from coarse clays, was manufactured. To the south of Frijoles Canyon, the glazeware dominated trade across the warmer Riverine country of central New Mexico. An exception was along the high, colder mesas of that area, where gorgeous Black-on-white bowls, named after Chupadero Mesa, remained in vogue for generations. Salinas National Monument is in the Chupadero Black-on-white country.

By A.D. 1350, the initial political readjustment to another episode of mass migration had passed, and Classic Riverine society began to emerge. Immense, unfortified pueblos were built up in bottomlands along major rivers. These were surrounded by hundreds of outlying "field-

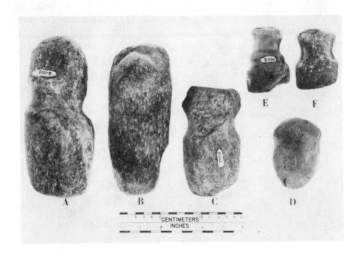

Stone axes from Bandelier area. E and F are of a distinctive Fibro-
lite stone traded into Bandelier from the Picuris area after about
A.D. 1400. Photo courtesy of the National Park Service, Bandelier
National Monument.

houses," used only during the agricultural season. Nothing
like a Chacoan political or economic network ever again
emerged. Each large pueblo became more like a miniature
city-state or a walled town of feudal Europe. As best we
know, primary loyalties were first to kin-based clans, then to
special religious and curing societies, and then to the village. Pueblos alternately cooperated and competed with one
another as circumstances dictated, much as the pueblos do
today.

The A.D. 1300s, 1400s and 1500s were a period of nearly
constant adjustments to local agricultural conditions.
Many villages went through several cycles of partial abandonment and renewal. Occasionally floods swept away precious bottom land, and local river districts were abandoned
altogether. It is rare when archeologists find a village that
was continuously inhabited for any great length of time.

Classic Riverine society produced significant accom-

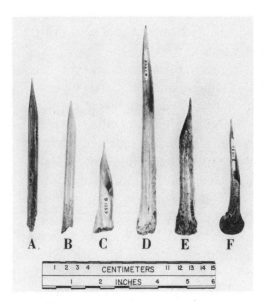

A B C D E F

| 1 2 3 4 | CENTIMETERS | 11 12 13 14 15 |
| 1 | 2 INCHES 4 | 5 6 |

Bone awls found at Rainbow House. Rabbit, turkey or deer bone was an important raw material for small tools throughout the ancient Southwest. Photo courtesy of the National Park Service, Bandelier National Monument.

plishments in technology, the arts, and religion. In addition to new techniques of pottery manufacture, a wide variety of more efficient tools was introduced to the Bandelier area. Beautifully shaped stone axes of unusual hardness were fashioned from large river cobbles. Some of these have ¾ - spiral hafting grooves—a more effective innovation for tightly securing the axe head. Even in modern times, an axe handle tends to separate from the head due to tremendous impact pressures and centrifugal forces created by the wide overhead swing favored by woodsmen the world over.

All manner of small tools were created from wood, bone, stone, and pottery. Wooden artifacts of this period usually have decayed, so archeologists most often find the more durable materials. Animal bone was used extensively for everything from whistles and small flutes to intricate sewing needles and sets of incising tools. Manos and metates were large and efficient, often set up in rows, or "mealing bins," where women gathered to talk and grind corn in a modest "assembly line."

Pottery reached new heights in form, style, and versatility. Everything from fired-clay pendants to tobacco pipes to elaborate miniature sets of finely painted bowls to *ollas* (larger kitchen vessels) was produced. Certain villages began to specialize in pottery manufacture, and much of what is known of fourteenth and fifteenth-century life around Bandelier is owed to microscopic analysis of the kinds of ground stone used to temper the clay used in pottery manufacture.

The technique of glazing pottery had been known in the Four Corners area since at least A.D. 400 or 500. Those early wares were Black-on-whites, glazed with iron silica, and tended to be short-lived. During the Classic Period, most of the various Rio Grande Glazeware styles used a lead-based glaze. Lead-bearing ores were obtained from deposits of galena and similar minerals from several nearby mining districts. The most important of these was near the present-day village of Cerrillos, about twenty miles southeast of the Pajarito, where turquoise has also been mined since prehistoric times.

Some of the earliest Rio Grande Glazeware, a type called Los Padillas Glaze-Polychrome, was produced at prehistoric Pueblo Camada on the Pajarito Plateau a few miles south of Bandelier. But, within a few years, two separate glazeware pottery traditions had evolved. The most widespread is characterized dark designs glazed on a red background, while the second, more limited in geographic distribution, produced glaze-on-yellow pottery. Both were handcrafted on the Pajarito Plateau, with the yellows more common south of the Monument.

By tracing the crushed stone used for tempering the clays, a rough outline of economics and changes in settlement can be be pieced together for the Bandelier area. In

84

Galisteo Black-on-white bowl. Riverine Period, about A.D. 1300 to 1400. Photo courtesy of Mike Marshall, Maxwell Museum Collections.

Jemez Black-on-white bowl. The Jemez area was one of the last strongholds of prehistoric Black-on-white pottery. Riverine Period. Photo courtesy of Mike Marshall, Maxwell Museum Collections.

Agua Fria g/Red. Early Riverine (A.D. 1300s) Period lead-glazed pot. Photo courtesy of Mike Marshall, Maxwell Museum Collections.

the A.D. 1300s, only Tyuonyi and Rainbow House in Frijoles Canyon produced glazeware. At the southern end of the monument, San Miguel Pueblo (LA 370) and Yapashi, near the Stone Lions, produced glaze-on-yellows.

Tyuonyi's glaze-on-reds were often tempered with crushed red volcanic scoria, a stone still commonly used in landscaping throughout northern New Mexico. But Tyuonyi's pottery did not enjoy much trade over any great distance. By the late A.D. 1300s, the focus of Rio Grande society had shifted eastward to Santa Fe and the Galisteo Basin.

In the mid-fifteenth century, new glazeware appeared and the southern Pajarito Plateau, including Pueblo San Miguel within the Monument, was largely abandoned. Only the pueblo of Kuapa (LA 3444), farther to the south on the Rio Chiquito, continued to be a center of population. Yapashi, probably founded sometime in the mid-1200s, no longer produced pottery and was no doubt in the process of abandonment. That left only Tyuonyi and Rainbow House producing glazeware with crushed tuff tempers form deposits in the Monument itself.

To the north of Frijoles Canyon, Otowi began to produce its first glazeware in quantity, replacing earlier Black-on-whites. No one is certain when Otowi was first founded. An earlier "component" undoubtedly lies beneath the huge pueblo of the late A.D. 1400s to mid-1500s, but only a few tree-ring samples have ever been analyzed from the partially excavated village; these date from mid-fifteenth to sixteenth centuries. Tsankawi, on its spectacular mesa in the northern part of the monument, also expanded rapidly during the earlier part of this time.

Pottery studies will eventually allow us an even more detailed reconstruction of the Classic Period on the Pajarito Plateau, but the basic facts are these: after A.D. 1300, the

Cieneguilla glaze polychrome bowl. Early Riverine (A.D. 1300s) Period. Photo courtesy of Mike Marshall, Maxwell Museum Collections.

Glaze "E" or "F" Rimmed bowl found at Jemez. Late Riverine (A.D. 1500s) Period. Note "runny" lines in design. This is typical of pots glazed near the end of the Riverine Period as ancient lead bearing deposits were mined to exhaustion. Photo courtesy of Mike Marshall, Maxwell Museum Collections.

Potsuwi-i incised pot. Riverine Period, about A.D. 1450-1550. Common on the northern Pajarito. Photo courtesy of Mike Marshall, Maxwell Museum Collections.

Jemez Pueblo. Photo by Carlos Vierra, 1913. Courtesy of Museum of New Mexico, negative number 42053.

true focus of Classic Period society moved east out of Bandelier. Only Tyuonyi and Rainbow House in the north and San Miguel and Yapashi in the south contained large populations, as most of the smaller sites in higher elevations above the Rio Grande were abandoned. Then, sometime in the early to mid-1500s, population concentrated at sites like Otowi, Tsirege, Puye, and Tsankawi on the far northern Pajarito Plateau. Tyuonyi and Rainbow House had already been abandoned by this time.

The Riverine Period is more complex than many textbooks indicate. Several major reorganizations and episodes of mass population movement had taken place before the Spanish arrived (1598). Between A.D. 1425 and 1450, and again in the mid-1500s, serious droughts forced major episodes of abandonment, followed by relocation and rebuilding in areas where farmlands were abundant. Bandelier and the Pajarito Plateau, like the high mesas above modern-day

Jemez Pueblo, were a safety valve of sorts—an upland area rich in game, valuable obsidian, and seasonal crops of berries, acorns, and pinon nuts, where entire clans could take refuge in times of drought or of conflict.

Unlike earlier periods in Southwestern prehistory, nearby lowland pueblos never again divorced themselves from adjacent mountain retreats. Although the pueblos in Bandelier had been completely abandoned before Spanish colonization, succeeding Indian peoples continued to use the Pajarito, worshipped within its confines, considered it part of their rightful territory and venerated it as "home." Even religion changed during the Classic period, as the Kachina cult, masked gods associated with rain, flourished. Kiva murals reached a zenith in beauty and symbolism and in complex, graphic portrayals of religious characters and events. Even petroglyphs, or "rock art," were laboriously hand-pecked in the recognizable "Rio Grande style." Many of these petroglyphs can still be seen at Bandelier.

This sense of homeplace is very difficult for non-Indian Americans to understand. Daily life was rich and varied, but always arduous. Men worked the soil and were weavers and craftsmen in stone. Women cooked, made pottery, tended to the annual replastering of houses, and cared for children. Men were heavily involved in kiva society and the ritual life of the village. Women formed the fabric of homelife and of nurturing the several generations under one roof. There was a sharp division of sex roles, but there was no real division between *sacred* and *secular*. Religion was not merely a Sunday event, a few hours of reverence in the midst of an everyday world. Rather, daily life and region were constructed quite like an onion: it took many layers of each to produce the complex whole of Puebloan society.

These traditions continue in modern times. Indian peoples still hold the Stone Lions sacred. Archeologists and

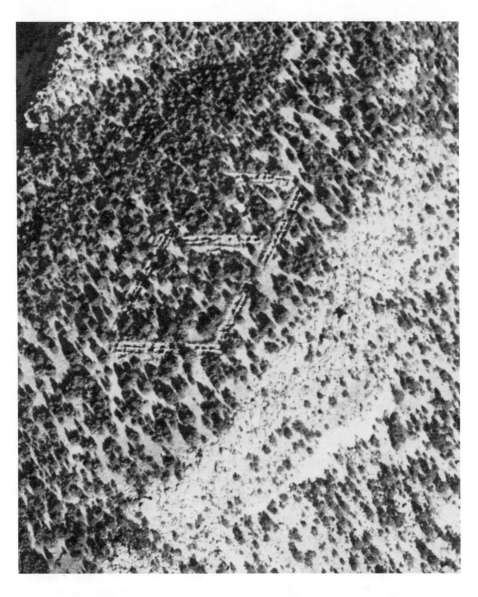

Aerial photo of Old Cochiti taken in 1989. Such villages, ancestral to
the modern pueblos, were often on mesas or bluffs overlooking the
modern sites. Photo courtesy of Baker Aero Works—Tom Baker,
1989.

Cochiti Pueblo. Photo by John K. Hillers, 1880. Courtesy of Museum of New Mexico, negative number 2493.

visitors consider the Stone Lions a "site," but the pueblos consider them a shrine; they come quietly and reverently to this sacred high place. In Pueblo religions many mountains are sacred. The Lions are best considered an altar within a great natural cathedral. Indeed, the Lions themselves, like many other shrines on the Pajarito, are a source of power and of hope. It took both to survive six hundred generations of uncertain life in and around Bandelier, but it was done. No other National Monument has such intimate connections with the remote past, the present-day Tewa and Keresan Pueblo peoples, and with their yet unborn generations. It is truly a place where yesterday, today, and tomorrow still coexist.

Part III

GIFTS FROM THE PAST

Close-up of Long House Ruin in 1964. Photo courtesy of National
Park Service, Bandelier National Monument.

Tyuonyi

The ruins of Tyuonyi (Chew-OHN-yee) are the archeological centerpiece of Bandelier National Monument. Probably founded in the late thirteenth century, much of what the visitor now sees was built between A.D. 1350 and 1450 in at least several distinct stages of construction.

This village is a rough, masonry oval similar to others, like Soldado Ruin west of El Morro, which were founded about the same time. Tier upon tier of rooms were built around the central plaza until the Pueblo assumed its final form. Some archeologists believe that the final building episode involved construction of the narrower tiers, only three or four rooms deep, which face Frijoles Creek. These tiers, they argue, transformed Tyuonyi into the enclosed oval that may be seen today.

We may never know precisely because this ruin was excavated between 1908 and 1911 by the legendary Edgar Lee Hewett, who founded the School of American Research and the Laboratory of Anthropology in Santa Fe. In those days, the modern dating techniques essential to a recreation of a pueblo's expansion, room-by-room, were still unknown. Roof beam fragments, collected thirty years after Hewett's excavations, were analyzed and dated by the University of Arizona's Laboratory of Tree-Ring Research—the world's authority on tree-ring dating, but those beam fragments accurately date only a few rooms. Those originally from upper floors are mixed in with those from the lower floors (built first), and sound roof timbers were often reused several times to build a succession of Anasazi structures. Perhaps one day, when the time is right, the National Park Service will authorize archeologists to investigate the still unexcavated portion of Tyuonyi where the contemporary trail through the ruin exits over ancient walls.

Tyuonyi looking south. Note absence of cliff rooms on north face of
Frijoles canyon. Frijoles Creek in background. Photo courtesy of the
National Park Service, Bandelier National Monument.

Six hundred years ago Frijoles Creek was much closer to the ruin's south walls than it is today. In fact, long-ago floods may have taken away some of Tyuonyi's southernmost walls. In its day, Tyuonyi was rather like a fortress. Only a narrow entryway to the east opened to the great plaza. Plaster made of mud and ash covered the masonry walls, and access to most ground-floor rooms was by ladder to the roof, then down through rooftop openings.

At its zenith, Tyuonyi's more than four hundred rooms, three kivas, and retaining walls along the creek created an impressive village. Pottery was manufactured locally for many generations. Though Tyuonyi did not have economic influence over a large geographic area, it was on an important frontier between Tewa-speakers to the north and Keresan speakers, who claim it today as one of their ancestral homes. Tyuonyi is still remembered in the rich oral traditions of both peoples, but its strongest ties are with modern Cochiti Pueblo.

Another unexcavated pueblo of about twenty rooms lies between Tyuonyi and the Big Kiva. Its precise age is unknown. The Big Kiva, between the ruins and Visitor's Center, was last repaired in A.D. 1513. Though no one knows just when Tyuonyi was abandoned, the early to middle sixteenth century is a likely period, since the village did not produce pottery after that time. Tyuonyi is particularly impressive when viewed from Ruin Overlook, on the mesa above it, and when winter snows highlight its intricate outline on the floor of Frijoles Canyon.

Rainbow House

One-half mile downstream from Tyuonyi, Rainbow House (LA 217) rests on the north bank of Frijoles Creek. Several excavations at this medium-sized pueblo indicated soft earth nearly five feet below the current ground surface, which means the site is probably atop an earlier ruin. It was named by the Keresan Indians who assisted in the 1948 excavations.

Rainbow House consists of two blocks of rooms: the larger block contains forty-six rooms; the smaller, known as the plaza Unit, has nine comparatively large rooms. A kiva lies just to the eastern edge of the plaza. Rainbow House was first mentioned by Adolph Bandelier, but was not excavated until the late 1940s. It was undoubtedly founded somewhat later than Tyuonyi. Like other sites in the area around Frijoles Canyon, it contained both Biscuit wares, thought to be ancestral to Tewa pottery, and Rio Grande glazeware.

Most of the corn recovered during excavations was described as a small-cobbed, twelve-rowed Chapalote, quite like the early Archaic varieties widely grown before the first century A.D. Rainbow House (elevation 6000 feet), contained little of the larger eight-rowed pueblo corn grown at the large Classic Period pueblos along the Rio Grande at elevations of about 5200 feet.

It must have been inhabited during much of Tyuonyi's zenith, but archeologists know little of the interaction between the two neighboring pueblos. A major building episode took place between 1448 and 1451. Was Tyuonyi building at the same time? Like Tyuonyi, Rainbow House was also made of volcanic tuff blocks, mortared in adobe; well-finished floors were of plastered mud bound into a durable clay by adding small amounts of animal blood.

Long House ruin in 1912 on the south-facing wall of Frijoles Canyon. Note good preservation in parts of ruin. Photo courtesy of the National Park Service, Bandelier National Monument.

Unlike Tyuonyi, there were no stone-lined floors, a hallmark of "rodent proof," ground-floor storage rooms.

A wide variety of Classic Period artifacts were recovered from Rainbow House during excavation. These include many implements of turkey, deer, and rabbit bone. The material for finely-shaped basalt manos, or grinding stones, originally came from the lower mesas near the Rio Grande. Beautiful axes of fibrolite, a hard, dense stone found high in the Sangre de Cristo Mountains north of Santa Fe, were also recovered. Arrowheads were usually made of the prized, local obsidian, but small scrapers, knives and spokeshaves were fashioned from black basalt found near the mouth of Frijoles Canyon. Rainbow House was probably abandoned at about the same time as Tyuonyi.

Long House ruin in 1964. Note erosion of some cave rooms in the cliff face when compared to 1912 photo. Photo courtesy of the national Park Service, Bandelier National Monument.

Long House and Talus House

Talus House is nestled against the north cliff face of Frijoles Canyon above Tyuonyi. Its shallow, shadowed cave (cavate) rooms were originally the back rooms of upper stories, gouged out of the cliff with stone hand-tools. Below lies Talus House, reconstructed to give the visitor an idea of what a small cliff-house was like seven hundred years ago. During the 1930s it was rebuilt from local tuff blocks, and even the original holes for roof beams, which had been picked into the cliff-face hundreds of years ago, were re-used. Judging from pottery collected below Talus House eighty years ago, it appears to have been renovated again

Talus House. Reconstructed by archeologists using a crew of San Ildefonso stonemasons in the 1920s. Photo courtesy of the National Park Service, Bandelier National Monument, 1966.

and again in ancient times. Exact dates are unknown, but it was probably not used much before A.D. 1200, and quite likely was lived in until Tyuonyi was abandoned. In 1909, Edgar Lee Hewett referred to this cliff ruin as "Sun House," a name not used in many years.

Long House is approximately one-quarter-mile upstream from Tyuonyi. It is the largest, longest, most complex house on the Pajarito Plateau. Here about eight hundred feet of soft cliff face supported nearly three hundred rooms, some three-stories high. The roof beam, or *viga*, sockets dug into the cliff face are particularly noticeable. It too was rebuilt several times, but no modern studies of its artifacts have been undertaken since it was excavated in the early 1900s. It had its own kiva and could have housed a population of several hundred.

Frijolito Ruin

On the south mesa overlooking Tyuonyi lies Frijolito Ruin. Never fully excavated, it is sometimes said to be contemporary with Rainbow House. More likely it was founded in the late twelfth century or a little later; it is typical of the larger, more complex "Santa Fe Black-on-white Pueblos" which survived a century or so into glazeware times. It was undoubtedly abandoned before Tyuonyi and Rainbow House. It contains between seventy and eighty rooms and, as at many other Santa Fe Black-on-white sites, no ceremonial kiva is visible. Its heyday might have matched Tyuonyi's greatest period of growth (A.D. 1350-1450) or it might have been linked to Long House or Talus House.

Ceremonial Cave

High on the north cliff face, nearly a mile upstream from Tyuonyi, is a spectacular, reconstructed kiva inside Ceremonial Cave. To reach the cave, actually a large rock overhang, one has to scale the canyon walls to a height of nearly 150 feet above Frijoles Creek, a breathtaking experience. Inside the rock overhang there were once nearly thirty small masonry rooms, in places two stories high. Dug into the floor was a small kiva, entered from the roof; now reconstructed, it gives the visitor a good idea of a local kiva.

For generations, archeologists have been confused by the details of kiva construction on the Pajarito. When excavated, many evidence a complex combination of "local experimentation," with other features similar to kivas of the Chacoan and Mesa Verde country. Using these details, archeologists once sought to unravel the "when and where" of the various migrations to the Pajarito after A.D. 1100. Most likely it will require far more excavation on the Pajarito and far more attention to precise dating of ruins before there are definitive answers—even then much may remain as tantalizing conjecture. Most scholars agree that features of both Chaco and Mesa Verde kivas show up on the Pajarito, but kiva details vary from one to another even in one village, as demonstrated at the various sites in Frijoles Canyon.

The Ceremonial Cave kiva is small and simple, like many others in the northern Rio Grande Valley. Since the cave's location was the one most easily defended in all of Frijoles Canyon, it was probably built about A.D. 1200 during the heyday of similar (easily defended) cliff palaces throughout the Southwest. Later cliff dwellings on the Pajarito were often less well situated for defense. Directly below and

"Ceremonial Cave," named by Edgar Hewett in early 1900s. It was a habitation site with associated kiva. Photo courtesy of the National Park Service, Bandelier National Monument.

across the canyon floor on the south side of Frijoles Creek lies a small Pueblo III ruin. First noted by Bandelier and called House of the Water People, it is ten to fifteen rooms in size, unexcavated, and seldom mentioned. It probably was built about the time of Ceremonial Cave. It contains traces of the red and black polychromes from western New Mexico and early Santa Fe Black-on-white pottery fragments. No kiva is obvious at House of the Water People, so it may be an early pueblo with close connections to Ceremonial Cave.

Yapashi and the Stone Lions

Yapashi Pueblo lies atop the mesa south of Alamo Canyon. It is quite a trek from the Visitor's Center, but a worthwhile one for hiking enthusiasts. Alamo Canyon is south of the Monument headquarters, separated from Frijoles Canyon by Lummis Canyon. Here the vegetation changes from the ponderosa found around Tyuonyi to pinon-juniper parkland.

Yapashi Pueblo is also regarded as an ancestral home by modern Cochiti Indians. Edgar Lee Hewett excavated here briefly in 1908, but no adequate report was ever published. From pottery found here, he dated the site between A.D. 1200 and 1475. Much of its glazeware appears to have been trade goods from San Marcos Pueblo in the Galisteo Basin and from Tonque Pueblo between Albuquerque and Santa Fe. We now know more about the dates of pottery manufacture than did Hewett, and this suggests that Yapashi flowered between A.D. 1350 and the late 1400s. Yapashi is a Keresan name that refers to the sacred enclosure around the Stone Lions. It was quite large, several stories tall, with hundreds of rooms, and was probably an important Keresan village just before the southern Pajarito Plateau was abandoned in the early 1500s.

The Stone Lions, one-quarter-mile west of and slightly above Yapashi, have long been revered by pueblo peoples. Whether they were first purposefully carved, or were natural tuff boulders resembling the mountain lions and given careful finishing touches, is irrelevant. The twin, reclining figures are actively venerated, and Indian peoples make pilgrimages to the site. It is said that young Zuni men still make the pilgrimage on foot—a rite of passage into manhood and traditional Zuni religious life. From Zuni, it is a round-trip of about four hundred miles.

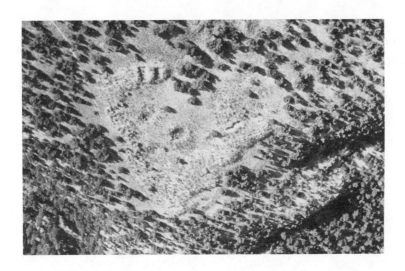

Aerial view of Yapashi within Bandelier National Monument. Photo courtesy of Baker Aero—Tom Baker, 1989.

Yapashi, photo probably taken by Charles Lummis, late A.D. 1800s. The walls no longer stand this high. Photo courtesy of the National Park Service, Bandelier National Monument.

Stone Lions as the shrine appeared in 1964. Photo courtesy of the National Park Service, Bandelier National Monument.

Stone Lions as the shrine appeared in November of 1988. Note evidence of current religious offerings. Photo courtesy of Andrea Sharon.

Painted Cave

Painted Cave is about two and a half miles down Capulin Canyon from the Pueblo of Yapashi and its Stone Lions. The cave, like Ceremonial Cave, is actually a large, recessed rock overhang. It too opens up towards the south. It may once have contained masonry rooms, but the floor is now bare. There were cave rooms below the painted chamber when Adolph Bandelier first described it in 1880.

Unlike much prehistoric rock art on the Pajarito, the art work here is painted, rather than the more common engraved petroglyphs. Its many designs are often superimposed, but one can still make out horned-serpents associated with the water gods, stars, various kachina masks, stepped cloud designs, and human figures. Capulin Canyon is much dryer than Frijoles and the landscape more like that of the Rio Grande district several miles to the east.

Capulin Canyon is believed to have been densely inhabited at one time, but few intact ruins have been formally investigated. Pottery fragments found nearby span the period from about A.D. 1150 to 1500, so it is hard to tell just when the cave was painted. Judged by the style of designs and the superimposed artwork, many of the surviving paintings date between A.D. 1300 and 1600. Several designs were painted after Spanish arrival in the area, since one stylized human figure is depicted on horseback.

Pictographs in "Painted Cave," Capulin Canyon. Photo courtesy of the National Park Service, Bandelier National Monument.

Tsankawi

The ancient pueblo of Tsankawi is, like Otowi, in a detached section of Bandelier Monument. It lies one and a half miles east of New Mexico Highway 4 where it forks towards Santa Fe. This northern area is very rich in pueblo ruins, and Tsankawi is among the most spectacular.

Its four large roomblocks are arranged in an irregular rectangle around a central plaza, with nearly a dozen kivas at the site. It contained between 350 and 400 rooms and, like others nearby, was built of hand-cut volcanic tuff, mortared with adobe. Portions of Tsankawi were once several stories high. Photographs taken a century ago show how deterioration of such ruins has accelerated in modern times.

Tsankawi was one ancestral village of modern-day Tewa speakers. The name "Tsankawi" is contracted from a longer Tewa name (saekewikwaje onwikege) meaning "village between two canyons at the clump of sharp, round cactus." Deep trails worn into the Pajarito's volcanic bedrock by the many generations of Indian occupants still lead to the ruin. For visitors who have never seen such "foot-carved" trails, this ruin is worth the walk, which takes about two hours round-trip. Its mesa-top setting is impressive: cactus (mostly cholla) still grows there, along with sharp, narrow-leaf yucca; and from the ruin, one can see much of the surrounding mesa country. Like other late, Classic Period pueblos on the Pajarito, Tsankawi is in the pinon-juniper zone, away from the ponderosa.

Tsankawi gave its name to a distinctive Tewa Black-on-cream pottery and, although not adequately dated, flourished in the A.D. 1400s and 1500s. Most of its farmlands and the faint remains of small, one- or two-room "field" houses, typical of the Classic Period, are in the canyon bottoms surrounding Tsankawi's mesa.

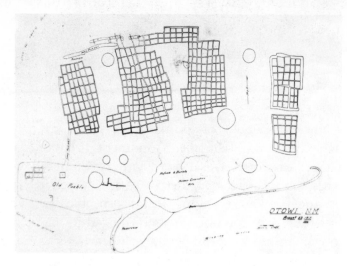

Site plan of Otowi Ruin on the Pajarito Plateau. Plan done by
Lucy W. L. Wilson about 1915. Courtesy of Museum of New Mexico, negative number 81911.

Otowi

Otowi is one of the few late, magnificently large Classic
Period pueblos on the Pajarito. It lies about one and a half
miles north of Tsankawi. At one time or another, it has been
either in or out of the Monument boundaries, depending
on government land trades. But it is integral to the Monument's saga, and so is included here. Its setting is quite striking. To the untrained eye, it looks like a huge, grassy hillside
which is "lumpy." The lumps are actually the five enormous
walled roomblocks, now decayed and filled with wind-
blown soil. Huge pockmarks indicate its ten circular kivas
and reservoir. Never properly dated or systematically excavated, Otowi (also called Potsuwi'i in older texts) was a late
center of Classic Period population on the Pajarito.

Otowi sits atop a local vantage point on the ridge which
separates Pueblo Canyon from Bayo Canyon. Cave rooms,
like those at Frijoles Canyon, line the south-facing tuff cliff
to the north of the site. Otowi's burial ground was partially
excavated by Edgar Lee Hewett in 1906. Some grave offer-

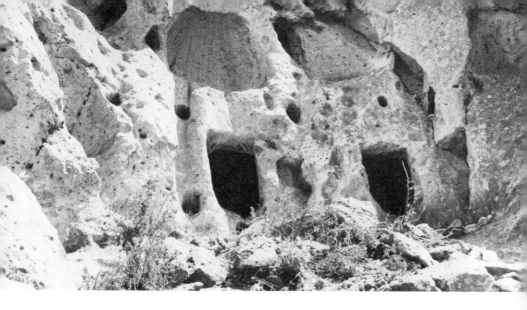

Cliff dwelling at Otowi Ruin on the Pajarito Plateau. The cliff faces south. Photo courtesy of Museum of New Mexico, negative number 41997.

ings found were spectacular: beautiful polychrome bowls, glazeware, and loosely-woven cloaks of turkey feathers and rabbit fur, which once were used as "thermal" blankets.

Much of the pottery found there is late Rio Grande glazeware. The later glazeware often had "runny" designs, for as generations of Indian miners worked their way deeper into the lead deposits at Cerrillos, the lead content became higher and the glaze's melting point was lowered. The lower melting point created runny lines because the glazed lines prematurely melted upon firing. In other parts of Otowi ruin, earlier Santa Fe Black-on-white pottery has been found in small quantities. That early pottery, coupled with the reservoir, typical of late A.D. 1200s Upland villages, causes some archeologists to believe it was founded in the Upland Period—a Tewa stronghold to which people returned in numbers a century or so later. It was inhabited until about A.D. 1600 when the northern Pajarito and the Chama Valley were abandoned for uplands to the south and east near Albuquerque.

Grinding and cooking implements typical of the late Upland Period. Photo courtesy of the National Park Service, Bandelier National Monument.

Other Gifts from the Past

There are hundred of other ruins on the lands of Bandelier National Monument to enjoy, but prehistoric American Indian society has given the modern world much more than fascinating stone ruins. Some of today's food and clothing is also a legacy from the past. Common Pajarito items such as domesticated turkey, corn, "pinto" and "kidney" beans, squash, tobacco, sunflower seeds, watermelon, chilis, and domesticated cotton have all found their way into our own everyday lives. Bandelier visitors wearing cotton clothing and contemplating a summer meal of barbecued turkey, corn-on-the-cob, baked beans, and watermelon are enjoying modern strains of agricultural products once carefully tended in tens of thousands of long-forgotten gardens. Ancient Indian America is much more than a tourist attraction; its accomplishments are the basis of many sectors of our modern economy.

Suggested Readings

Bandelier, Adolph F.
1946   *The Delight Makers.* Dodd, Mead & Co.: New York.
       (popular reading)

Cordell, Linda S.
1984   *Prehistory of the Southwest.* Prentice-Hall: Englewood Cliffs, N.J.
       (general audience)

Hoard, Dorothy
1983   *A Guide to Bandelier National Monument.* Los Alamos Historical
       Society: Los Alamos, N.M.
       (general audience)

Jennings, Jesse D. (editor)
1983   *Ancient North Americans.* W. H. Freeman & Co.: New York. See
       especially chapter 10 by William D. Lipe, "The Southwest," pp.
       421-494.
       (college level textbook)

Lange, Charles H., and Carroll Riley
1966   *The Southwestern Journals of Adolph Bandelier 1880-1882.* Univer-
       sity of New Mexico Press: Albuquerque, N.M.
       (general audience; annotated for scholars)

Ortiz, Alfonso (Volume 9 Editor)
1979   *Handbook of North American Indians, Vol. 9: The Southwest.*
       Smithsonian Institution: Washington, D.C.
       (the standard reference work in the English-speaking world)

Stuart, David E.
1985   *Glimpses of the Ancient Southwest.* Ancient City Press: Santa Fe,
       N.M.
       (popular audience)

1985   "Prehistoric Pajarito." *New Mexico Magazine*, vol. 63, no. 1, Janu-
       ary, pp. 92-100.
       (popular audience)

Stuart, David E. and R. P. Gauthier
1988   *Prehistoric New Mexico*, 2nd ed. University of New Mexico Press:
       Albuquerque, N.M.
       (technical, college-level reference)

Index

About the Author

David Edward Stuart first came to New Mexico, and to Bandelier, in the winter of 1967. He earned his Ph.D. in anthropology from the University of New Mexico in 1972, taught briefly in Florida, then returned to UNM as a founding staff member of the Office of Contract Archeology. During the 1960s and 1970s, he conducted field work in Alaska, Mexico, South America, and his native Appalachia.

From 1977 to 1987, Stuart was a consulting anthropologist in Albuquerque. Between assignments he published a wide variety of works—from textbooks to magazine articles—on anthropology and Southwestern archeology. Best known are various editions of the technical reference, *Prehistoric New Mexico* (1981, 1984, 1988), written with R. P. Gauthier, and *Glimpses of the Ancient Southwest* (Ancient City Press, 1985).

David lives in Albuquerque near the University of New Mexico, where he is Assistant Vice President for Academic Affairs and teaches "Ancient Man in New Mexico" each fall. He lectures annually at Bandelier National Monument and is an award-winning writer. He enjoys receiving mail from his readers. Feel free to write him, care of Ancient City Press.